50$^+$ Programs
for Tweens, Teens, Adults, and Families

50+ Programs

for Tweens, Teens, Adults, and Families

12 MONTHS OF IDEAS

AMY J. ALESSIO,
KATIE LAMANTIA,
AND EMILY VINCI

ALA Editions

CHICAGO 2020

Extensive effort has gone into ensuring the reliability of the information in this book; however, the publisher makes no warranty, express or implied, with respect to the material contained herein.

ISBN: 978-0-8389-1945-3 (paper)

Library of Congress Cataloging-in-Publication Data

Names: Alessio, Amy J., author. | LaMantia, Katie, author. | Vinci, Emily, 1988- author.

Title: 50+ programs for tweens, teens, adults, and families : 12 months of ideas / Amy J. Alessio, Katie LaMantia, Emily Vinci.

Other titles: Fifty plus programs for tweens, teens, adults, and families

Description: Chicago : ALA Editions, [2020] | Includes bibliographical references and index. | Summary: "This programming guide offers interactive events for tweens, teens, millennials, and adults as well as families. A section on themed club programming is also included." —Provided by publisher.

Identifiers: LCCN 2019027214 | ISBN 9780838919453 (paperback)

Subjects: LCSH: Libraries—Activity programs—United States. | Young adults' libraries—Activity programs—United States. | Libraries—Marketing.

Classification: LCC Z716.33 .A4355 2020 | DDC 025.5—dc23

LC record available at https://lccn.loc.gov/2019027214

Cover design by Alejandra Diaz. Images © Adobe Stock. Text design by Kim Thornton in the Museo and More Pro typefaces.

♾ This paper meets the requirements of ANSI/NISO Z39.48-1992 (Permanence of Paper).

Printed in the United States of America

24 23 22 21 20   5 4 3 2 1

Contents

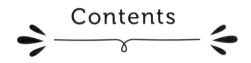

Introduction

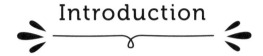

WELCOME TO *50+ PROGRAMS FOR TWEENS, TEENS, ADULTS, AND FAMILIES:* *12 Months of Ideas.* We have collected ideas for programming for five different groups of participants in this guide: tweens, teens, millennials, older adults, and families. Most programs collected here have variations to make programs appeal to different groups.

While arranged in a monthly format to help planning throughout the year, many of these programs are interchangeable with different months.

The second section offers programs in themed club format, with tips on hosting meetings and recommendations for fun activities. New ideas for clubs that are introduced in *A Year of Programs for Millennials and More* are also provided.

How to Use This Book

The ideas for each topic are broken down into manageable portions. Many ideas are listed under each program theme so that libraries may choose the ones that work best in different communities. Details for each program are provided under the following headings where appropriate.

PREP TIME
This section includes planning and shopping as well as setup time.

LENGTH OF PROGRAM
This time is a suggestion for a stand-alone event, but more time may be needed to include all activities.

NUMBER OF PATRONS
This is a suggestion for the maximum number of people attending to make the activities most enjoyable. For example, craft programs should have fewer people if instruction and help will likely be needed.

SUGGESTED AGE RANGE
This book offers programming suggestions for tweens (ages 10–13), teens (14–19), millennials (20–39), older adults (40+), and families. *Families* means "intergenerational

groups with caregivers, grandparents, and youth." Unless specified, if a program is recommended for millennials, it is not necessarily relevant for all adults. Teen programs may not work with tweens in many cases.

SUPPLIES/SHOPPING
This section lists the items needed for the event. Activities and variations may include additional materials.

ACTIVITIES
This section explains how to run the program and includes some setup tips and ideas for experiences to include in programs. Crafts are also included here.

TRIVIA AND OTHER FREE GAMES
These are easy ways to engage participants in the topic or to build interest before the event.

MARKETING
This section includes techniques and tips for displays and other advertising for each event.

VARIATIONS
Ideas for adapting similar programs for different age groups as well as suggestions for ways in which to alter a program slightly to give a different experience will be found here. Is there an aspect of this theme that tweens in particular may enjoy? Is there a way to change the setup of this program to make it enjoyable for the whole family? If there is a way to add something to the event to make it more enjoyable for different age groups, that will be found here also.

PRO TIP
Specific or unusual ideas will be added to this section for several programs to enhance and simplify events.

part I

A Year of Ideas

chapter 1

January

THE WEATHER MAY be cold and dismal, but exciting programs at the library will help ensure that this is a memorable year for patrons young and old. In **Community Connections**, millennials will discover groups around the area that may help them with jobs, social networking, or personal wellness. Or the library will go out into the community and meet people of all ages at area events. At the **Entrepreneur Fair**, interested tweens, teens, millennials, and older adults will see skills that could translate to successful businesses for them. They will also connect with the financial and technological aspects of running their own small businesses. **Game Design** brings teamwork and skills together as tweens and teens create intricate boards of fun. Finally, **Rememberlutions** is a terrific family activity that helps everyone remember special moments throughout the year.

Community Connections

Invite organizations, local businesses, and young professionals to a networking event hosted by your library. This is a great opportunity for people to learn about businesses and organizations in their communities and resources in their personal or professional lives and how these can enhance their careers.

PREP TIME	LENGTH OF PROGRAM	NUMBER OF PATRONS	SUGGESTED AGE RANGE
4–5 hours	2 hours (drop-in)	50	Millennials

SUPPLIES/SHOPPING

- bottles of water
- coffee
- tables
- signs for each company
- chairs
- nametags
- pens

PRO TIP

The Community Connections Fair is best scheduled for the evening or weekend because many people have daytime jobs or school.

ACTIVITIES

- Reach out to local organizations and businesses and invite them to a networking event at the library several months ahead of time. Recruit businesses and organizations from the local chamber of commerce and discuss the goals of this program and what both parties would like to see as outcomes. While this is not specifically a job fair, it could be beneficial to people seeking a new job in their local community. This is also a great way to showcase the library's resources to help job seekers, so include brochures and signage that illuminate the many resources your library has. If you have a business librarian (or reference librarian), set aside time to present information about how the library can assist job seekers and businesses.

- Compile a list of businesses and organizations present to offer to patrons. Include the mission, values, and goals of the organization or business, as well as job openings (if applicable). Create tabletop signs for each business or organization. Check in with the participating businesses and organizations one week prior and confirm their attendance. On the day of the program, set up one table per organization or business around the perimeter of the room and a few empty tables in the center for discussion/networking. Allow young professionals to circulate the room and meet with people who may be interested in their skills or how different organizations can help their professional development. If another room is available, use that room for mentorship interviews and one-on-one networking.

- Get involved with the community and set up booths about the library at local events and organization meetups. Be prepared with key information such as how to get a library card, upcoming program handouts or guides, and resources the library has to offer. If there are specific resources or topics, make sure to tailor your information or handouts to the topic and audience.

- Meet the people where they are and hold a program at a local organization. This can be as simple as doing a book talk at a school board meeting, demonstrating how to use a database at a local government agency's office, welcoming new businesses at a chamber of commerce event, or providing simple crafts at a night-out event. Being active and engaged with the community increases the presence, awareness, and value of the library.

MARKETING

- Use the participating organizations' logos (with permission) to advertise.
- Share the online or paper flyer with the chamber of commerce and participants to advertise the event.
- Create a book display with networking tips, interview skills, job advice, local history, and so on.

VARIATIONS

- *Older Adults:* Design a senior services program around the exciting offerings local organizations have for senior citizens and providing support for their caregivers. This can include fitness classes, volunteer opportunities, health services, or cultural meetups. Make sure to advertise your library's services for the homebound, technology classes, and activities or book discussions held at senior centers.
- *Family:* Invite local attractions in the area that are family friendly and host an open house. Patrons can see what suits their family's needs and budget. This is a great way to learn about new or forgotten treasures in your community.

Entrepreneur Fair

Patrons of all ages may be interested in starting or growing businesses. Technology offers new ways of going into business, and the library is the intersection of plans and action for businesses. Help patrons come up with new ways to turn good ideas into lucrative businesses. Described here as a daylong festival with workshops, this could easily be broken up into programs throughout a month with follow-up networking sessions.

PREP TIME	LENGTH OF PROGRAM	NUMBER OF PATRONS	SUGGESTED AGE RANGE
5 hours to contact speakers, 1 hour to set up rooms on the day of the program	1-day festival or weekly options	30 per session	Tweens, teens, millennials, or older adults—programs focus on different ages in a day- or monthlong festival

SUPPLIES/SHOPPING

- coffee, tea, bottled water
- snacks

ACTIVITIES

- *Idea Fair:* Invite local business owners to have booths in the lobby or another high-traffic area for a two-hour festival. Be sure to have variety, from shop or salon owners to home or cottage industries. All business owners will have the chance to advertise, but they should provide a sheet with information about what their business is and when it started, with tips for someone who wants to start a similar business. They should also be prepared to answer questions. Throughout the week before the festival, each business owner could be highlighted on a screen in the library or on the library website.

> **PRO TIP**
>
> People can be at different stages of thinking about starting a business or growing a business. Advertise that the reference desk can research anything from markets and customer bases to finding suppliers with a thirty-minute appointment or through online reference options.

- *Creative Business Demonstrations:* Invite patrons to apply to demonstrate a skill that led to their business, from jewelry making to cake decorating to website design, in thirty-minute workshops. These could be open to teens and up. Information on food and business licensing could be handed out to participants.

- *Turning Skills into Cash for Teens:* Some workshops could be aimed specifically at teen entrepreneurs age thirteen and up, such as first-aid babysitting CPR instruction, website or graphic design, YouTube editing, and social media income. Teens who work at their own or other small businesses could be invited to discuss what they do and how they built their business.

- *Small Business Licensing:* Invite members of the chamber of commerce, small business association, and a local accounting firm to discuss setting up a small business.

- *Entrepreneur How-To:* Collect information from people who attend the fair on what topics they would like to see in depth. Show patrons how the library can support small businesses with workshops on needed topics—for example, basic website design or simple marketing graphics.

- *Virtual Businesses:* Offer a workshop on how to market and develop skills to make money online. Local experts may be needed as speakers, including local authors, experts in social media sites such as Pinterest, or digital graphic artists. Include time highlighting resources the library has such as directories on publications that pay for writing or artwork.

TRIVIA AND OTHER FREE GAMES

- *Get to Know Local Businesses:* Invite local businesses to offer a special to patrons who show their library cards prior to the entrepreneur fair. Or offer a punch-card system where patrons who show a receipt or something signed from five local businesses get fines cleared or another reciprocal bonus.

MARKETING

- Local businesses involved in the programs could advertise the library events with a handout listing all participating businesses and all available programs.

VARIATIONS

- *Work from Home Opportunities:* Invite local community college or continuing education instructors to discuss ways parents can reenter the workforce or keep skills current with working from home.
- *Entrepreneur Networking or Club:* If there is a lot of interest in small business topics, offer a regular networking event for small business owners and a guest speaker on rotating topics.

Game Design

Whether it's a hobby or possible career track, game design is an arena more accessible now than ever before. A game design program introduces patrons young and old to this activity in a no-pressure setting that inspires them to learn, create, and play. Depending on patron interest, this can be turned into a club with regular meetings to keep the inspiration/creativity flowing and progressing!

PREP TIME	LENGTH OF PROGRAM	NUMBER OF PATRONS	SUGGESTED AGE RANGE
4–5 hours	1 ½ hours	15	Tweens and teens

SUPPLIES/SHOPPING

- white printer paper
- crayons/markers/ colored pencils
- pencils
- rulers
- scissors
- old magazines
- dice

ACTIVITIES

- *Partnerships:* Consider partnering with a local community college or university/ art school to put on this program. Game design clubs as well as game design students may have a particular interest/willingness to help out. Another place to look for partnerships is local game and comic shops. Many already hold dedicated gaming events and may perhaps host meetings of game design clubs.

- *Using Python in Game Development:* Python is a programming language that can be used to create simple video games and is a great entry point for interested patrons. Inquire to see if someone on your staff is familiar with using Python and its potential in game design and could assist with this program.

- Individually or as a group, storyboard a game with elements such as a goal, characters (if it's a video game), and challenges players may face. Participants can draw different screens (again, in the case of a video game) and put them in order of how a player will progress through the game. Based on the interests of the group, you could also do this as one big group activity, working on one game and melding together everyone's different ideas and contributions. Another option is to start out this way, and if some of the patrons want to work on their own ideas, they can focus on those while you continue to lead the group. In addition to sketching out ideas using the materials provided, participants may have ideas to add materials and complete games at home.

MARKETING

- Be sure to advertise this program near the library's video game collection as well as in your teen department.
- Additionally, see if local game stores and comic shops will allow you to hang/distribute flyers in their establishments too.

VARIATIONS

- Though video gaming is likely what comes to mind when one thinks of game design, it's not the only option. A board game design program or card game design program also incorporates creativity, logic, and storytelling skills.

Rememberlutions

With the New Year comes New Year's resolutions, which can be daunting to many of us. Rememberlutions are an alternative/addition to the kickoff of a new year. They are, essentially, notes jotted to oneself throughout the year commemorating moments both big and small that a person wants to have the opportunity to look back on. In this casual, crafty program, you will help your patrons create a jar in which they can keep their Rememberlutions throughout the year.

PREP TIME	LENGTH OF PROGRAM	NUMBER OF PATRONS	SUGGESTED AGE RANGE
1–2 hours	2 hours (drop-in)	25 (depending on supplies)	All ages (great family program)

SUPPLIES/SHOPPING

- mason jars (various sizes, no smaller than one pint)
- fabric in various colors/patterns (optional: precut into 5 × 5″ squares)
- ribbon in various colors and patterns
- fabric paint, chalkboard paint
- sponge brushes, paint brushes
- stickers
- cardstock (various colors)
- scissors
- hot-glue gun

ACTIVITIES

- *Create Your Rememberlutions Jar:* Separate the two parts of a mason jar lid. Using the inner part of the lid, trace a circle on a piece of fabric of your choice. Cut the circle out and hot glue it to the inside of the outer ring of the lid. Set it aside to dry while you decorate your jar. Decorate the outside of the mason jar using fabric or chalkboard paint, stickers, and ribbon—however you wish! Once your jar is decorated, attach the lid and carefully cut a one-inch slit in the fabric.

MARKETING

- Display a finished Rememberlutions jar with index-card sized Rememberlutions that include information about the program at the service desk in each department (kids, teen, adult).

VARIATIONS

- *Tweens and teens:* Rather than creating a Rememberlutions jar, create a Rememberlutions notebook or journal! Participants can decorate the front of a composition book using Mod Podge and items cut out from old magazines or books, as well as stickers and paint. As an additional option, participants can use the inside of the notebook to list items they are looking forward to in the coming year. (Be sure to remind participants to leave space to add more!)

chapter 2

February

BOOST SPIRITS IN February with **Floral Mood Boosters**. Flower crafts including pressed flower bookmarks and sachets help patrons think of spring. **Medieval Magic** has enough activities for a day of fun for different ages at the library, including a castle contest, catapult construction, and shield design. **More Mardi Gras** helps patrons celebrate without going to New Orleans with crafts and a hide-the-baby (plastic, of course) treasure hunt in the library. And finally, a **Salty and Sweet Fest** pairs flavorful combinations with interactive fun in a twist on traditional Valentine's sweets and chocolate programs.

Floral Mood Boosters

By February, many people are thinking about spring and looking forward to it. For those planning gardens or those who are simply sick of winter, plan some floral-themed events that offer history, education, and fun.

PREP TIME	LENGTH OF PROGRAM	NUMBER OF PATRONS	SUGGESTED AGE RANGE
3 hours	1-hour workshops or a full day of fun events	25 for crafts	Teens, families, millennials, or older adults

SUPPLIES/SHOPPING

Paper Flowers
- origami paper
- double-sided wrapping paper or construction paper

Pressed-Flower Bookmarks
- parchment paper
- iron plus board or place to iron
- small flowers such as violets
- cardstock cut into bookmark strips
- craft liquid glue

Indoor Gardening
- small plastic or glass containers
- dirt
- seeds for herbs, small flowers, or vegetables, such as peppers or mums
- scoop to transfer dirt

Sachets
- nylon tulle circles or squares (craft stores sell these in bulk for bridal favors)
- narrow ribbon (craft stores sell spools of these; six inches at least will be needed per item)
- dried floral bits with different types of flowers

ACTIVITIES

- *Meaning of Flowers:* Make a handout of flowers with their meanings and small pictures if possible.

- *3-D-Printed Flowers or 3-D Pen:* Feature technology with flowers for this event by showing how to design and print simple flower shapes with library technology. If everyone wants a flower from the printer, they can pick up designs later: www.designsharemake.com/design/flowers.

- *Paper Flowers:* Invite people to try to make paper flowers, either rolled roses or origami tulips. These videos provide instructions and examples:
  - » Rolled roses video: www.youtube.com/watch?v=SeN9_K1xrWQ
  - » Origami tulips video: www.origami-instructions.com/origami-traditional-tulip.html
  - » Plenty of other how-to videos can be found online

- *Indoor Container Flowers:* This activity can be used to start plants that can be transferred to an outdoor garden later or to make terrariums. Discuss types of plants that can be started indoors before growing outside and lighting that can be used indoors. A speaker from a gardening club can assist. Or invite audience members to choose a container and a seed to plant. For the terrarium, glass containers can be filled with dirt and seeds. Small toys or seasonal decorations can enhance terrariums.

- *Pressed-Flower Bookmarks:* Flowers have to be flattened between parchment-paper squares, using a big book. Then they can be ironed completely flat (without steam!), before being glued on to the bookmarks. A website with terrific directions on pressing the flowers, then attaching them to bookmarks, can be found here:
  - » www.greetingsofgrace.com/pages/how-to-press-flowers
  - » www.greetingsofgrace.com/pages/how-to-make-a-pressed-flower -bookmark

- *Sachets:* A small amount of dried flowers can be placed in the center of the tulle before being gathered with a ribbon and double-knotted.

TRIVIA AND OTHER FREE GAMES

- "Match the flower to the meaning" is a fun handout that can help advertise the program.

MARKETING

- Post cards with facts about the meaning and use of flowers across several countries on a bulletin board. This site has many fascinating facts: www.living language.com/blog/2017/03/21/the-meaning-of-flowers-cultural-traditions -in-giving-flowers.
- You could also create a flower craft bulletin board. Invite families and youth in the library to try making paper or tissues flowers and attach them to the board to advertise the floral program.

VARIATIONS

- Each activity listed here can be adjusted into programs for different ages in other months of the year. For example, the sachets and bookmarks work for teens and tweens who may want to make gifts for themselves or for Mother's Day in May.

Medieval Magic

Enjoy traveling back through time at a medieval festival at your library with crafts and engaging demonstrations.

PREP TIME	LENGTH OF PROGRAM	NUMBER OF PATRONS	SUGGESTED AGE RANGE
6 hours	3-hour festival	30 for craft sessions, unlimited for fair and demonstrations	Families

SUPPLIES/SHOPPING

Castle Contest
- prizes
- cardboard play castle

Catapult Contest
- Popsicle sticks
- Dixie cups
- elastic hair bands
- rubber bands
- glue
- small rubber balls

Choker Craft
- purchased velvet chokers
- charms—sun, moon, stars, and fleur-de-lis
- large silver jump rings
- long-nosed pliers

Juggling Demonstrations
- small balls or oranges
- nylon scarves or plastic bags (grocery store)

Archery
- toy archery play set with suction-cup or Velcro-tipped arrows

Cross-Stitch Bookmark and Calligraphy
- markers
- thick cardstock, cut into bookmarks
- blank writing paper

Shield Design
- wooden play shields (ordered online or from a craft store)
- acrylic paint
- brushes
- bowls for water
- paper towels

ACTIVITIES

- Set up stations throughout the library for demonstrations during the festival. A meeting room or two could be used for certain crafts and speakers.

- *Strolling Characters:* Invite members of the Society for Creative Anachronism or local theater groups to attend the festival in costume to mingle with patrons.

- *Weapons History:* Hire weapons (swordplay guilds) or fencing experts to offer a program at the library with demonstrations.

> **PRO TIP**
>
> Actors with armor may be available in places near Medieval Times restaurants or renaissance fairs. They could give talks about fashion, weapons, and life in this time period.

- *Pleasing Pies:* Invite a baker or food history expert to discuss the different styles of crusts and tarts used in baking in medieval times to today. Make a handout with recipes and a list of books in the library for attendees. If possible, purchase small tarts to taste.

- *Castle Contest:* Invite patrons to send in photos of creative castles they have built with Legos or cardboard. Put photos online or on a poster in the library to advertise an upcoming medieval festival. Purchasing a play castle for the youth area will also help advertise. Keep it near a service desk to help it last. Or invite youth and tweens to draw and design their dream castles on paper.

- *Archery with Velcro:* Let young children try a toy archery kit in the youth area.

- *Choker Craft:* Take registration for up to twenty-five people, ages thirteen and up, to make choker necklaces. Order premade velvet chokers online in bulk, and offer a selection of charms. Demonstrate how to attach the charms with silver jump rings to the necklace. The rings can be opened with long-nosed pliers. Then slide the charm on and close the ring over the velvet band so it slides easily. Display materials on medieval designs and clothing or the history of jewelry to enhance patron interest.

- *Bookmark and Calligraphy design:* Families, millennials, and teens may enjoy designing bookmarks that look like needlepoint. Make samples of medieval tapestries and embroidery stitches, and invite people to use markers to make similar designs on precut bookmarks.

  » Show samples of fonts and letters from medieval times, such as those shown at Medieval Chronicles (www.medievalchronicles.com/medieval-life/%EF%B B%BFmedieval-calligraphy), and invite patrons to try making those letters with markers.

- *Catapult Contest:* Take registration for families or youth ages twelve to eighteen for a catapult contest. Place craft materials on a table, and give participants twelve minutes to make a catapult that can launch a superball. At the end of the time period, see which catapults can launch the balls the furthest at a designated, cleared area.

- *Coat of Arms:* Take registration for twenty-five participants for this fun project. Families or youth ages eight to fifteen can design and paint a coat of arms on a shield. Offer materials with the meaning of symbols and samples of what the crests may look like.

- *Juggling Lessons:* Invite an expert to show families how to do simple juggling, or have online tutorials running on a screen, where patrons can try to juggle in wide spaces with scarves or plastic bags. With an expert or a skilled instructor, patrons could try to juggle oranges or balls.

TRIVIA AND OTHER FREE GAMES

- *Match the Symbol to the Meaning*: Make displays of materials about medieval times in several areas of the library in the two weeks prior to the festival. Fiction and nonfiction items can be featured. Place a simple trivia game on displays that asks patrons to match the coat-of-arms symbol to its meaning. Patrons of any age who complete the game will be entered in a drawing for a prize. Prizes could include being named the king or queen of the festival, complete with inexpensive crowns, or a coupon to clear fines at some time in the future.

MARKETING

- *Calligraphy Wall*: Make a poster with a calligraphy alphabet and invite patrons to try to write their names with markers on Post-its to put on the wall.

More Mardi Gras

Mardi Gras history and fun can travel north of Louisiana with these crowd-pleasing crafts and activities. You can even utilize makerspaces and special technology with Mardi Gras–themed fun.

PREP TIME	LENGTH OF PROGRAM	NUMBER OF PATRONS	SUGGESTED AGE RANGE
4 hours, including shopping	Several 1-hour programs for one weekend day or across the week before Mardi Gras	25 for craft classes, unlimited for some drop-in events	Teens, millennials, and families

SUPPLIES/SHOPPING

Fleur-de-Lis Keychain
- purple, green, or gold materials for 3-D printer
- keychain hardware (craft stores)
- two-inch head pins
- wire cutters
- long- and flat-nosed pliers
- silver jump rings—at least one-half inch

Paper Crown or Mask Making
- precut masks or crowns
- markers
- optional: metallic stickers or small stick-on gems

Mask Making
- velvet masks (bought in bulk online or in craft stores)
- fabric glue
- flat gems
- feathers
- metallic sharpies

Themed Jewelry
- bulk gold-toned or colored ribbon organza necklaces
- gold-toned charms of masks or fleur-de-lis
- Gold jump rings, at least three-eighths-inch in diameter
- Long-nosed pliers

Hide the Baby
- small plastic babies in a variety of skin tones
- small prizes
- plastic or cardboard treasure chest
- bead necklaces

Tote-Bag Decoration
- fabric glue
- fabric markers or Sharpies
- canvas tote bags, purchased in bulk
- ribbon in gold, purple, and green

ACTIVITIES

- Set the stage at the library in the two weeks prior to Mardi Gras. Run movies set in New Orleans, such as *The Princess and the Frog* or *The Big Easy* (older viewers), and set out displays of jazz or zydeco music and Cajun and southern cooking books and fiction.

- Feature your makerspace or new technology with themed projects, including

  » *Fleur-de-Lis Fun:* Offer demonstrations in how to design a fleur-de-lis keychain with the 3-D printer. Take registration for twenty tweens, teens, or families, and print several out ahead of time. Each design must have a circular closed tab to attach the ring and keychain hardware. Families can learn how 3-D printing is handled at the library and how it works with design software before putting their keychain together.

  » Demonstrate how to make fleur-de-lis, crowns, and mask shapes with shape cutters in the library makerspace if available. Or else invite patrons of all ages to draw and cut out shapes to put on a poster. The poster will be the "library Mardi Gras float," and patrons can use tape or glue to attach their shapes to decorate the float.

  » *Crown and Mask Designs:* Youth and families can do drop-in paper crown or mask designing with precut kits. Metallic stickers or even small stick-on gems could be used or simply coloring materials.

  » *Mask Making:* Take registration from tweens, teens, or millennials for a fancy mask-making workshop. Patrons can glue beads and feathers onto velvet masks or decorate them with metallic Sharpies. Consider playing jazz music and offering slices of king cake, if available in your area, or moon pies.

  » *Themed Jewelry:* Take registration from teens, millennials, or adults to make Mardi Gras–themed choker necklaces. Using long-nosed pliers, patrons can open jump rings and attach a charm before closing the ring over the chain or organza necklace.

  » *Hide the Baby:* Hide a few different plastic babies in baggies with a note instructing the person who found it to return it to the youth or teen service desk. The person who finds it gets a strand of beads from the treasure chest and gets to hide the baby again. (They should let staff know where.)

  » *Tote Decoration:* In honor of floats that throw decorated purses at Mardi Gras, offer a workshop for ages thirteen plus on using the shape-cutting machines. Participants can glue shapes onto tote bags and also decorate with markers and ribbons.

  » *Jazz Music Demonstration:* Invite local high school or college groups to play jazz music during the weekend before Mardi Gras or the evening of Fat Tuesday.

TRIVIA AND OTHER FREE GAMES

- *Phrase to Meaning:* Make a list of Mardi Gras and New Orleans terms and match them to their meanings, like Muffuletta to sandwich.

MARKETING

- Hang beads from service desks, and hand them out at all participating Mardi Gras events. Staff should also wear them in the weeks before the programs.

VARIATIONS

- *Millennial Mardi Gras Party:* Invite young adults to participate in a Mardi Gras party with king cake, beads, music, and nonalcoholic drinks. Crafts included in the More Mardi Gras programs could also be done during the party.

Salty and Sweet Fest

Sea salt and caramel. Chocolate pretzels. Bacon and dates. Prosciutto and melon. Sweet and sour chicken. Fries and shakes. These combinations are popular for a tasty reason! Invite patrons to indulge in new flavorful combinations of snacks along with some fun activities.

PREP TIME	LENGTH OF PROGRAM	NUMBER OF PATRONS	SUGGESTED AGE RANGE
2 hours, including shopping	1 hour	30	Tweens, teens, millennials, or older adults

SUPPLIES/SHOPPING

- rubber gloves
- paper plates
- water and cups
- napkins

Chocolate Fondue
- fondue pot or microwave
- spoons
- milk-chocolate chips
- half and half
- pretzels
- ridged potato chips
- plain popcorn
- cooked bacon (optional)

Caramel Strawberries
- caramel sundae sauce
- strawberries
- sea salt

Popcorn Flavors
- plain popcorn and buttered popcorn, prepared
- cinnamon
- honey
- chili powder

Prosciutto and Melon
- prosciutto, cut into strips
- honeydew and cantaloupe, cut into bite-sized pieces

Meatballs
- one can chili sauce (any kind)
- one cup grape jelly
- Crock-Pot
- frozen meatballs

Trail Mix
- assortment of nuts
- sandwich baggies
- spoons
- coconut
- dried apricots or other fruits
- tiny M&Ms
- sunflower seeds
- bowls

Optional
- Chex mix in at least two flavors, including one with chocolate (optional)
- variety of potato chips in different flavors
- popcorn-flavored jelly beans (Jelly Belly)

ACTIVITIES

- *Chocolate Fondue:* Mix the milk chocolate chips and half and half into a fondue pot or in a microwaveable dish until the chips are melted. Put some chocolate on plates along with a small serving each of pretzels, potato chips, popcorn, and bacon. Ask patrons to rate the flavor combinations.

- *Caramel and Strawberries:* Cut strawberries in half and put some on patrons' plates. They can drizzle caramel sauce on their berries and add sea salt if desired.

- *Popcorn Flavors:* Put some plain and buttered popcorn on patrons' plates. Invite them to try combinations with the cinnamon or chili pepper seasonings. They can also try drizzling honey to see if it improves either popcorn flavor.

- *Potato-Chip Tasting (Teens and Tweens):* Put a few chips of each flavor on teens' plates. Have them vote on favorites and rank by saltiness. Be sure to read the salt percentages from the labels along with fat content for informational value.

> **PRO TIP**
>
> Do not choose more than four different types of things to taste (or four of the previous activities) in a one-hour program, and keep encouraging everyone to drink water in between activities.

- *Chex Mix (Millennials and Older Adults):* This is similar to the potato-chip tasting idea. Put different types of Chex Mix on plates and invite patrons to rank favorites. Optional: hand out recipes for Chex Mix (www.landolakes.com/recipe/20421/the-original-chex-party-mix/).

- *Make Trail Mix:* Put bowls with coconut, assorted nuts, sunflower seeds, tiny M&Ms, and dried fruits along with spoons on a table. Give patrons sandwich baggies and invite them to make their own trail mix.

- *Meatballs (Millennials and Older Adults):* Mix a jar of chili sauce plus one cup of grape jelly in a Crock-Pot and add frozen meatballs on high for an hour before the program begins. Have spoons available to serve from the pot.

- *Prosciutto Strips and Melon (Millennials and Older Adults):* Put strips of prosciutto and samples of honeydew and cantaloupe on plates. Invite patrons to wrap strips around melons to taste.

MARKETING

- Hand out copies of the original Chex Mix recipe on cards with the program information on the back at the reference desk or place them in cookbooks on a display.
- Have a Twitter or Facebook poll with favorite sweet and salty combinations to start a thread about the program.

VARIATIONS

- *Teens and Tweens:* Play Bean Boozled or have teens taste different flavors of jelly beans (including popcorn) at another program to advertise this one.

chapter 3

March

SPRING MAY BE coming, but in many areas, the weather is still cold and wet. This chapter balances fun indoor events with tips on getting ready for spring. **Austenland** takes fans of the romantic author back in time as participants revisit books, movies, and television interpretations of the classic novels. **Green Everywhere** will help even those people who think they kill plants find a way to nurture a plant indoors or start vegetables to plant outside in warmer weather. Tweens, teens, and millennials will enjoy learning and tasting in **Healthy Twists to Snacks** as they make easy-to-create recipes. And teens can look forward further to summer with a **Teen Job Fair** that helps interested teens find openings in the community for summer employment.

Austenland

Jane Austen's books have touched countless hearts for centuries. The cultural touchstones of Jane Austen's characters have connected and resonated with people throughout the ages and will continue to do so for years to come. Celebrate this amazing author and her works with an Austen-themed program.

PREP TIME	LENGTH OF PROGRAM	NUMBER OF PATRONS	SUGGESTED AGE RANGE
4 hours	1 hour	20–30	Older adults

SUPPLIES/SHOPPING

British Treats
- scones
- clotted cream
- jam
- plastic knives

Cucumber Sandwich Ingredients
- bread
- cucumber
- cream cheese (8 oz.)
- ¼ c. mayonnaise
- ¼ tsp. garlic powder
- ¼ tsp. onion salt
- dash of Worcestershire sauce
- measuring cups: ¼ c.
- measuring spoons: ¼ tsp.
- bowl
- spatula

Regency Games
- multiple card decks

Regency Dancing
- English country dance music
- open space
- microphone

Austen Presentation
- computer or DVD player
- screen
- presentation system
- Austen movie of choice

Tea Time
- kettle (electric or standard with stove)
- variety of loose tea (Darjeeling, Earl Gray, English Breakfast, chamomile, etc.; tea bags can be substituted for loose tea)
- milk
- sugar
- spoons
- teacups
- tea strainer

ACTIVITIES

- At the center of almost every situation in Austen's novels, there is tea involved. Learn about the history of tea and how to create it the British way. Use a kettle instead of a microwave (a big no-no in British culture) to heat the water. Let the water boil, but do not keep it boiling. Add loose tea to the water to infuse the

> **PRO TIP**
>
> Reach out to the Jane Austen Society of North America (www.jasna .org) and see if there is a local chapter in your area. They may have contacts or ideas that could be beneficial to your program.

flavor. Pour into teacups, making sure to add a strainer to each cup before pouring so leaves do not get into the teacup. Sample different varieties of tea and ask patrons which one was their favorite. Another option is to do a tea-tasting quiz. Pour a few different varieties into kettles or teapots and ask patrons to guess the flavor of each tea. Encourage patrons to describe the tea they are tasting (dark, smoky, fruity, etc.) and discuss the history of tea.

- Sample different treats that you would normally find in an Austen novel: scones, jam, clotted cream, biscuits, cucumber sandwiches, and so on. Many of these novelty items can be found at international stores or online. If there is a bakery, café, or restaurant in town that offers or can offer these treats, see if they are interested in partnering with the library. Alternately, you can offer a Jane Austen baking class and teach patrons how to make items they would read about in an Austen novel. Cucumber sandwiches require little prep work and can be eaten immediately without any baking required. Cut the crusts off a loaf of bread; wash and peel the cucumber. Thinly slice the cucumber and mix cream cheese, mayonnaise, garlic powder, onion salt, and Worcestershire sauce in a bowl until smooth. Spread the cream-cheese mixture on each bread slice and place cucumber slices on top of the bread slices. Sprinkle lemon pepper on the cucumber and place the bread slices together. Cut the sandwiches in half so they are shaped like triangles and serve them as delicious finger food. Source: www.allrecipes.com/recipe/220775/english-tea-cucumber-sandwiches.

- "So what do you recommend to encourage affection?" asked Mr. Darcy. "Dancing. Even if one's partner is barely tolerable," replied Elizabeth Bennet. While affection is not necessary for this English country dance program, an open mind and willingness to learn are. Offer an English country dancing lesson for beginners—no partner, costume, or experience necessary. Partner with a local dance studio or check online to see if there is a local English country dance group available to teach this style of dance or beginner's steps.

- Create a travel presentation around Jane Austen's life and books in Britain. There are a multitude of options to create an engaging presentation: life in Georgian England in the eighteenth to nineteenth centuries; landmarks in her works and life; customs, food, and culture; and so on. Incorporate pictures, maps, drawings, and statistics about the life and times of Jane Austen. This is an exciting learning opportunity for both you and your patrons and will help give context to her novels.

- Incorporate Jane Austen's novels into a book club, either already existing or new. Options for your book club (or Jane Austen's book club) are limitless. Reading her six published novels is a great start, but there are many variations possible. Incorporate a biography of Jane Austen, nonfiction novels about the Austen fandom, or variations of her novels by other authors: *Pride and Prejudice and Zombies*, *Mr. Darcy Takes a Wife*, *Death Comes to Pemberley*, and so on. Design an entire book club around Jane Austen or theme an existing book club for a year or more.

- Screen Jane Austen (or Austen-themed) movies at the library as a series program. This can include the BBC *Pride and Prejudice* miniseries, any film version of her novels, or movies based around the Austen fandom, such as Austenland or Jane Austen's Book Club. Check to make sure your library has proper licensing to screen the chosen movie(s). Invite patrons to stay for a discussion after the movie.

TRIVIA AND OTHER FREE GAMES

- Create trivia questions or quizzes themed around Austen's life, books, or even a single book. Incorporate movie or television adaptations questions.
- Play card games mentioned in Austen's novels: whist, piquet, cribbage, cassino, loo, and more. Check out Geek and Sundry for inspiration: https://geekandsundry .com/games-favored-by-the-ladies-and-gentlemen-of-jane-austens-novels.

MARKETING

- Tie-in your Jane Austen–themed program by aligning it with a memorable moment in Austen's life or in one of her six books. Celebrate Jane Austen on her birthday (December 16, also known as Jane Austen Day) or the publication date of one of her novels.
- Use Jane Austen's silhouette portrait and create flyers or bookmarks that advertise the library's event. Include famous quotes from her novels and place them in her books on the shelf.

VARIATIONS

- *Family:* Host a tea party for families or parents and children. Encourage children to bring their stuffed animals or dolls. Play games from the Regency era, such as whirligig or Jacob's ladder. While not directly tied to Jane Austen, it is a good introduction to life in Regency England.
- *Teens:* Read YA adaptations of Austen's novels, such as *Prom and Prejudice*, *For Darkness Shows the Stars*, or *Prada and Prejudice* and their correlated Austen novels. Teens will also enjoy the tea tasting program as well.

Green Everywhere
Indoor Gardening

This drop-in program gets people thinking of spring as they plant seeds for indoor gardening.

PREP TIME	LENGTH OF PROGRAM	NUMBER OF PATRONS	SUGGESTED AGE RANGE
2 hours	30 minutes (drop-in)	25	Older adults or families

SUPPLIES/SHOPPING

- table coverings
- misting bottles for water (dollar stores)
- seed starter soil
- gardening tools (one set per group or table): small shovels
- Sharpie oil-based paint markers
- tomato seeds
- herb seeds, such as basil
- terra-cotta pots with draining hole and saucer (one tall and one small per person or family)

ACTIVITIES

- Invite attendees or families to use the Sharpies to decorate the plant pots.
- Using the tools, participants transfer dirt into the pots and plant the seeds about one inch into the dirt. Everyone should mist the soil to dampen without making it too wet.

TRIVIA AND OTHER FREE GAMES

- *Match the Tool to the Use:* Put various gardening and kitchen tools into a display case with numbers on cards next to each. Invite people to identify the use for each on a sheet. Draw a winner for a set of gardening tools randomly from those who enter.

MARKETING

- Invite patrons to send pictures of their indoor plants for a mini contest on social media channels. Draw winners for a gift certificate to a local gardening store or nursery from those who send in photos.

VARIATIONS

- Hand out seeds or have a table for decorating mini inexpensive flower pots in the lobby and at branch libraries for Earth Day.

—Healthier Twists to Snacks—

People are always looking for easy ways to eat healthier without buying expensive, unusual ingredients. Not everyone may want to puree cauliflower to eat instead of potatoes. While some of these fixes may be known to older patrons, it's great to review easy recipes that busy people can make for younger audiences. This is a cooking demonstration program, with some options if access to a kitchen is not available.

PREP TIME	LENGTH OF PROGRAM	NUMBER OF PATRONS	SUGGESTED AGE RANGE
3 hours to try recipes optional	1 hour	20	Tweens, teens, or millennials

SUPPLIES/SHOPPING

- sharp knife and cutting board
- access to oven and microwave
- paper plates
- napkins
- cooking sheets
- microwavable plate
- parchment paper

Oven Fries
- four large baking potatoes
- olive oil

Zucchini Chips
- zucchini
- salt

Popcorn Flavors
- plain popcorn
- chili powder
- cinnamon

Trail Mix
- coconut
- dried fruit
- raisins
- variety of nuts
- sunflower seeds
- sandwich baggies

Frozen Yogurt Sundaes
- frozen yogurt in pints
- strawberries
- blueberries
- crushed pineapple, drained
- bowls
- spoons

> **PRO TIP**
>
> Set up once for this event and offer it for different age groups throughout the day and evening.

ACTIVITIES

- *Oven Fries:* These will take the longest to bake. Set the oven for 450°F before beginning the program. Cut potatoes into eight long wedges and place on cooking sheet. Drizzle with oil and sprinkle lightly with salt. Cook for thirty minutes, turning over halfway through.

- *Zucchini Chips:* Use these directions: www.dinner-mom.com/zucchini-chips -microwave-or-oven. Cut zucchini into slices, sprinkle with oil, and microwave for five minutes.

- *Flavored Popcorn:* Invite participants to see if they like the chili powder or cinnamon sprinkled on their popcorn.

- *Trail Mix:* Participants will make their own bags of trail mix from healthy ingredients.

- *Frozen Yogurt Sundaes:* Everyone can add fruit to frozen yogurt for healthy alternatives to sundaes.

MARKETING

- Ask local park districts, gyms, and grocery stores to post information about this program.
- Invite the public to send links to favorite healthy snacks on social media channels to boost awareness of this event.

VARIATIONS

- Older Adults: Invite a chef or representative from a grocery store to discuss healthy cooking alternatives, possibly with demonstrations.

Teen Job Fair

Develop a teen job fair that specifically meets the needs of high school job seekers looking for their first job. Connect teens with potential employers who hire teens for part-time or seasonal work and are flexible with scheduling. Allow teens to access different workshops and learn how to build their résumés while highlighting library resources. This program will be an invaluable resource for teens and highlight the value of teen employment in your community.

PREP TIME	LENGTH OF PROGRAM	NUMBER OF PATRONS	SUGGESTED AGE RANGE
10 hours	2–3 hours	Unlimited, as many as program rooms will allow	Teens ages 15–19

SUPPLIES/SHOPPING

- folders
- bottles of water
- organizations' table tents
- computer or laptop
- one table per business
- two chairs per business
- presentation system
- printer
- video camera

> **PRO TIP**
>
> Make sure you have clear signage and directional information for patrons, especially if multiple events are occurring in different rooms or floors. This is a great crossover program with Résumé/Cover Letter Writing (When You Don't Have a Long Job History) in chapter 8.

ACTIVITIES

- Determine the time line for implementing your teen job fair, make sure it doesn't conflict with community or high school events (dances or major sporting events), and work out how many businesses/organizations and attendees your library can accommodate in one or two program rooms.

- Seek out local businesses and employers in your service area that are interested in hiring teenagers for part-time or seasonal positions with a cold call, e-mail, or advertisement in the library's newsletter (one or two issues before the date of the job fair). Have a representative from the library who can discuss open positions, job duties, work experience necessary, and so on. Business and organization participant ideas:

  » park district (camp counselors, lifeguards, birthday helpers)
  » local sports team
  » local restaurants and ice cream shops
  » grocery stores
  » retail stores

» swim instructors
» senior centers or nursing homes
» daycare facilities

- Begin reaching out to employers three to four months before the job fair. Franchises and large retail businesses often require permission from their corporate offices to participate. Confirm with businesses and organizations one to two weeks prior to the teen job fair. Make sure they are prepared with multiple job applications, information about open positions, and a laptop/tablet to direct people to their websites. Encourage business representatives to arrive one hour before the job fair to ensure that there is enough time for setup and troubleshooting if needed. Set up your teen job fair with one table and two chairs per organization or business, with tables lining the perimeter. Allow foot traffic to flow and make sure there is room for teens to interact with all the participants. Provide water bottles for business representatives, as they'll be doing a lot of talking with teens.

- Create a handout of participating organizations and their locations, websites, and contact information for teen job seekers. This is also a great resource to pass on to students who were unable to attend the fair. Provide handouts about current minimum wages and teen labor laws from federal government online sources and a résumé and cover letter template. Begin to put these items together a few weeks before the program. Purchase folders to contain the information and label the folders "Your Library Teen Job Fair 20_."

- Hold speaker sessions that are focused on teen job seekers. Reach out to community leaders, job ministry and networking groups, school counselors, the chamber of commerce, Toastmasters, and youth advocates for speakers. For ideas for speaker session topics, consider the following:

  » The dos and don'ts of interviewing: How important is eye contact? How should I shake someone's hand? Can I wear my hat to an interview?
  » Job applications: How do I fill this out? Who should I put as references?
  » Résumé building: What should I do if I don't have a lot of job experience? Can I put down school activities and extracurriculars?
  » Job-seeking resources: How can the library help me in my job search?

- Offer one-on-one sessions to help teens create a clean and informative résumé. You can build a résumé from scratch or revamp an existing one to reflect their goals, activities, and values. Create a signup sheet at the public service desk for twenty-minute slots in a reserved study room or quiet area of the library.

- Use mock interviews to help teens prepare for a real interview experience. Shake their hands and ask standard interview prompts:

  » Tell me about yourself.
  » Why do you want this job?
  » Tell me about a major problem you recently handled.
  » How has school prepared you for working this job or at this company?
  » What are your strengths and weaknesses?

- After the mock interview, discuss what the participant did well, where he or she struggled, and how to improve. If possible, film each interview to send to the teen later so he or she can assess mannerisms, facial expressions, and answers to questions he or she was or was not prepared for.

MARKETING

- Promote this program with high school guidance counselors at school visits, open houses, and career nights. Announce the teen job fair during morning announcements at schools. Include information about the job fair in the adult section of the library program guide to gain the attention of parents.

VARIATIONS

- *Teens:* Change up your teen job fair to discuss career choices that do not require a traditional four-year college degree. These can include skilled labor positions, emerging medical technology training programs, military opportunities, and internships.
- *Millennials and Older Adults:* Set up dedicated time for headshot photo sessions at your library. If your library has a green screen or digital production room, allow patrons to choose digital backgrounds. Warn people not to wear green and risk blending into the background. This can also be done with headshots in the stacks or by a solid-color wall. Create a sign-in sheet with e-mails to send their pictures, and in their first picture, have each patron hold up a whiteboard or piece of paper with his or her name in marker to match up correct pictures and e-mails.
- *Families:* Create a volunteer fair that the entire family can participate in. Invite community organizations and find a volunteer opportunity that matches each family. These can be community initiatives, one-day projects, or a committed weekly/monthly volunteer day.

chapter 4

April

APRIL CAN BE a busy month. Teens look forward to the end of the school year and activities such as prom, whereas US adults have a tax deadline. Adults can learn new skills about investing, budgeting, and how to record all those important events in their lives or their children's lives on social media. **Creating Your Story** breaks down how millennials and older adults can post creative and lovely documentation of life events on Instagram, Snapchat, and more. **Investing for Beginners** takes the fear out of finances with information about apps and different ways to save money. **Making Budgets Less Taxing** does exactly that. Investing and budgeting can be scary and complicated, and these programs will show patrons that they are not alone in those fears—and that there are practical ways to help sort those issues. And the library can help teens afford a special event with a **Prom Formal Wear Donation and Giveaway**. By working together with the community and making use of gowns that have only been worn once in some people's closets, this event can have a lasting impact.

Creating Your Story

Whether it's via Instagram, Snapchat, Twitter, or any number of other platforms, social media has given each of us the power to create our own stories and define our own moments. And as with all power, with it comes a degree of responsibility. The purpose of this program is not to preach about social media safety but rather to demonstrate the potential of using the social media tools at hand in a creative and impactful way.

PREP TIME	LENGTH OF PROGRAM	NUMBER OF PATRONS	SUGGESTED AGE RANGE
2–3 hours	1 hour	20	Millennials and older adults

SUPPLIES/SHOPPING

- Connect a tablet/smartphone to a projection system so that you can demonstrate with the apps in a way that the entire room can see.
- Don't forget to tell patrons ahead of time to bring their smartphones/tablets with them.

ACTIVITIES

- It may serve well to begin with a walk-through of the Instagram and Snapchat apps, covering their general uses/features before delving into the intricacies of each one and how to create stories with a purpose. The important thing to emphasize, of course, is the impermanence of Instagram/Snapchat stories, which disappear after twenty-four hours.

- Next, demonstrate how to create Instagram/Snapchat stories, and show examples of ones created by others. Use your library's account.

MARKETING

- Create an Instagram/Snapchat story using your library's accounts (if it has them) to market to your patrons who follow you on those platforms.
- If your library does not have accounts on those platforms, all is not lost! Get creative with a display that includes some analog stories to catch patrons' eyes and pique interest.

VARIATIONS

- *Tweens/Teens: Movie Making!* Hold a program for a younger audience in which they use Instagram stories to make minimovies. You can have them storyboard as a group and then actually create the movies as individuals or in groups. Once again, emphasize that these stories will disappear after twenty-four hours, which helps center the focus on what is most important to include.

Investing for Beginners

The term *investing* can be scary for young adults who want to save for graduate school or homes. But an introduction to investing, highlighting many of the accessible apps and accounts, can be informative and stress relieving for patrons.

PREP TIME	LENGTH OF PROGRAM	NUMBER OF PATRONS	SUGGESTED AGE RANGE
1 hour	1 ½ hours, including time for questions	45–50	Millennials

SUPPLIES/SHOPPING

- apps for a library device, including Robinhood and other savings-oriented apps to demonstrate
- a small raffle prize like a change counter (optional)

ACTIVITIES

- Briefly demonstrate the basic functions of popular savings apps, including Robinhood, with a laptop and projector. Some may require the establishment of an account to show features, but library staff can learn about the apps and discuss the features while showing the main screen as an option. Other apps offer ways for people to save small amounts of change into an account. Show ones that have been long established for this program.

- Invite a member of a local investment club or a representative from the SEC (Securities and Exchange Commission) to discuss types of investments and rules for small investment clubs.

- Invite a panel of local finance professionals to discuss the differences between types of beginning investments and retirement accounts.

PRO TIP

Offer this program during Money Smart Week and invite patrons to send in questions ahead of time on social media so speakers can prepare.

TRIVIA AND OTHER FREE GAMES

- Offer patrons a term-matching quiz as they arrive and draw a winner from those who fill it out for the small prize.

MARKETING

- Make bookmarks that look like play money that include program information to hand out with reserve items.
- Create a Post-it board of patrons' favorite money-saving tips near a poster about the event.

VARIATIONS

- Older adults may appreciate a program themed on college savings accounts and retirement accounts.
- *Investing 101 Club*: Over a series of programs, offer information on themed aspects of investing. For example, one session would provide ways to look up investments through library databases, and another would offer a speaker on types of short-term investments with varying levels of risk.

Making Budgets Less Taxing

Learning the importance of budgeting is valuable at any age, whether it's saving for that Xbox, paying off student loans, or strategizing to come up with a down payment for a house. Many libraries participate in Money Smart Week to provide their patrons with the tools to get a better handle on their finances, and whether or not your library is one of them, it is a worthy endeavor to provide a program for your patrons that can help their financial well-being.

PREP TIME	LENGTH OF PROGRAM	NUMBER OF PATRONS	SUGGESTED AGE RANGE
4–5 hours	1 hour	20	Millennials

SUPPLIES/SHOPPING

- laptop hooked up to a projector so that your attendees can see the examples/information you're providing
- paper
- pens

ACTIVITIES

- Consider bringing in a financial advisor or other trained professional to assist in leading the program. This person will also be able to answer questions that attendees may have that you may not feel comfortable trying to answer.

- *Creating a Budget Worksheet:* There are plenty of free examples online of how to create a budget worksheet that assists in keeping track of money in and money out each month.

- *Free Budgeting Apps:* Millennials love apps! Present (though be mindful not to specifically endorse) the free budgeting apps that are available. Attendees can try out apps on their own to determine what will work best for them.

- *Long-Term Money-Saving Measures:* Present some money-saving tips that are an investment in the beginning but will help your budget in the long run—things like getting a good coffee maker/travel coffee mug to cut back on takeout coffee or household items that are washable to relieve the habit of continually purchasing disposable goods.

> **PRO TIP**
>
> Cross-promote with a program on healthy eating/meal prep (see chapter 9), as the tips provided there are in line with saving money by reducing how much is spent on eating out.

MARKETING

- If your library is taking part in Money Smart Week, include this program in your promotions. Additionally, create a display of financial advisory books and include on it information about the program.

VARIATIONS

- *Tweens/Teens:* Demonstrate the importance of creating a budget by relating it to their priorities. You can use big-picture examples such as the average price of takeout coffee three to four times a week, extrapolated to how much that cost is per month, per year, and so on, compared to the price of gas, rent, and other living expenses.

Prom Formal Wear
Donation and Giveaway

Help teens in your community find the perfect dress, suit, or accessory for prom. Ask the public to search their closets (a great idea to tie in with spring cleaning!) and donate their formal wear to a worthy cause. Give teens the opportunity to celebrate this special moment in their high school lives without breaking the bank.

PREP TIME	LENGTH OF PROGRAM	NUMBER OF PATRONS	SUGGESTED AGE RANGE
8–10 hours	3 hours, can be repeated the next day if necessary	Unlimited as long as room can accommodate	Teens

SUPPLIES/SHOPPING

- coatracks
- room dividers (pipe and drapes)
- hangers
- safety pins
- yarn
- body-length mirrors
- tables (one to two for accessories)

ACTIVITIES

- Create a time line for accepting donations of formal wear from the community, designate a storage location, and set date(s) for the giveaway. Determine what types of formal wear you are willing to accept at your library for donations. For example, will you be accepting shoes, hairpieces, purses, pocket squares, cufflinks, and so on, or will you only accept clothing? You may want to consider including menswear (suits, tuxedos, vests, and ties) as well and marketing to teen boys. Don't forget to check the date of prom with the local high school to plan at least six weeks in advance.

> **PRO TIP**
>
> Sort the clothes into sizes when you receive them to save time organizing and adding tags later.

- Set up a consistent day and time for the public to donate their formal wear, and prepare staff to accept clothing. This will make the storage and organization process easier. A great way to implement this is to set up donation times on the Saturdays the month before the giveaway. This gives adults who work a weekday job multiple chances to donate their formal wear in case they miss a day, and staff will know the process for accepting and storing the donations.

- Determine how and where you are going to store and organize the donated items. Dresses and suits take up a lot of room! Borrow or use the library's coatracks until the giveaway, or allocate a program room or open staff space. Create homemade tags that have an S, M, L, or XL sizing (group items together—i.e., small = sizes zero to four, medium = six to ten). Use a hole punch to make a hole in the tag and then add a string through the punched hole and a strap of the dress, or add a safety pin and stick it through the tag to avoid damaging the clothing. Remove any items that are stained or extremely ripped. Purchase extra hangers if needed.

- Reserve room dividers several weeks in advance, and consider renting additional coatracks to display the formal wear. Create dressing rooms out of rented room dividers (drapes and pipes) in the program room, or use a reserved study room near the program room as a dressing room. Black out any windows in rooms that will be used for dressing rooms with construction paper ahead of time. Add long mirrors to dressing rooms or one directly outside of each room. Organize donated items by size, and add them to designated coatracks in the program room.

- Reach out to a local cosmetology school and ask them to demonstrate how to do simple updos and nail design. Provide fashion and hairstyle magazines for patrons who are waiting to get their hair done or peruse the formal wear. If possible, show movies about the high school prom experience, such as *10 Things I Hate about You*, *Never Been Kissed*, and *High School Musical 3*. Make sure you have a licensing agreement to screen them at the library.

- On the day of the program, allow ten to fifteen teens and parents into the room at a time to give them room to browse all the items. Station a staff member outside of the designated changing rooms to help with the flow of traffic. If you can repeat this program on multiple days (a Saturday and Sunday or a Friday evening and Saturday afternoon), this would be beneficial to teens who are involved in activities or sports. Allow each teen to take one piece of formal wear clothing and one to two accessories, depending on the stock and turnout.

- Plan to donate the remaining formal wear clothes to a local high school, especially if they have a fashion program, or a resale shop. Donation options can also include the Glass Slipper Project, Becca's Project, or Prom Girls Rock! which specialize in prom giveaways. Consider partnering with a neighboring library to share stock so teens in multiple communities can benefit.

MARKETING

- Advertise the formal wear donation guidelines and giveaway program in the adult section as well as the teen section of your program guide because many adults will be the ones to donate their formal wear or their children's. Place stickers or flyers cut out in the shape of dresses in between fashion and hairstyle magazines and books in your young adult collection. Advertise at local high schools and ask to promote during morning announcements.

VARIATIONS

- *Millennials:* Instead of hosting a prom formal wear giveaway, host a wedding formal wear giveaway. Ask for donations of wedding dresses, bridesmaid dresses, veils, suits, and tuxes. Offer ideas on how to save money on your wedding (e.g., how to create wedding favors, DIY updos, and more). Plan or promote with bridal shops, wedding planners, and local social media wedding groups.

chapter 5

May

THESE INVITING MAY programs offer helpful tips along with activities purely for family fun. **Basic Car Repair** can help patrons save time and money as they learn important skills. **Cooking with a Waffle Iron** shows easy recipes to get more out of beloved appliances, following a popular food trend. As tweens and teens head into the end of the school year and think about the future, **Middle and High School Survival Strategies** may help ease worries. A **Sing-Along Movie Night** will help the entire family with a relaxing social event. There is something for everyone this month.

Basic Car Repair

Learning how to perform basic car repair and maintenance is a practical life skill that many people will use at least once in their lives. Learning to drive is a major life milestone, and with that comes the responsibility of car upkeep and repair. There are numerous rewards in learning how to identify, diagnose, and trouble-shoot minor car issues, including financial savings and independence. By learning how to identify different parts of a car, change oil or a tire, or jump-start a car, you will be saving your patrons hundreds of dollars in the future and teaching them to be self-sufficient in a time of crisis. So prepare to get dirty as you demystify the inner workings of cars and get under the hood.

PREP TIME	LENGTH OF PROGRAM	NUMBER OF PATRONS	SUGGESTED AGE RANGE
4–6 hours	1–2 hours	10–15	Millennials

SUPPLIES/SHOPPING

- car (borrowed from staff or program partner)
- drop cloths

Jump-Start Supplies
- jumper cables
- additional car

Oil Change Supplies
- oil
- oil pans
- funnel
- wrenches of various sizes

Change a Tire Supplies
- wrenches of various sizes
- car jack
- spare tire

* Check for special parts needed that correspond to the automobile that will be used.

ACTIVITIES

Choose a myriad of different activities to help your patrons learn about proper car repair and maintenance that go along with being a responsible car owner. These activities can include identifying the inner workings of a car (engine, electrical system, transmission, etc.), changing oil or a tire, jump-starting a car, and educating your patrons about the proper disposal of parts and oil. If you or a colleague are not familiar or comfortable with auto repair, reach out to local car mechanics to see if they would be willing to partner with the library for this event.

CRAFTS, TRIVIA, AND OTHER FREE GAMES

- Find a blank car-engine diagram and ask patrons to identify different pieces of the car. Another option is to open the hood of your car and take a picture. Have program attendees take the identifying test in the beginning and end to see how much they learned.

MARKETING

- Create a display of Chilton's car repair books to advertise your program. Create a poll (online or physical) and ask patrons what car repair skills they have, if any. If you're partnering with a local car shop or school auto class, ask them to place flyers in their place of business or school.

VARIATIONS

- *Tweens:* Substitute basic car repair for basic bicycle repair. Teach tweens how to patch a tire, fix the chain, replace foot pedals, and so on. Partner with a local bicycle shop owner if there is one in your community. Tweens will also learn how to identify and use tools successfully in an area of their lives that affects them directly.
- *Teens:* Visit auto classes at a local high school and invite teens (with the supervision of a teacher) to teach the class to adults or other teens. This is a great way to get teens into the library and have them interact with adults to share their knowledge.

PRO TIP

If your library does not have a garage to perform this work, make sure you plan a backup date if there is inclement weather. Another alternative is to create a partnership with a local car repair shop or school and host an off-site program.

This program can be turned into a program series with new topics of car maintenance to cover during each session.

Cooking with a Waffle Iron

A current cooking trend is to try to cook different foods with the waffle iron. It's always good to get more use out of an appliance that takes up space in the kitchen, and the waffle iron is especially fun to try new things on.

PREP TIME	LENGTH OF PROGRAM	NUMBER OF PATRONS	SUGGESTED AGE RANGE
1 ½ hours, including shopping time	1 ½ hours	20–24	Teens, millennials, older adults or families

SUPPLIES/SHOPPING

- large electric waffle maker with four waffle-cooking surfaces to make demonstration foods or four to six small, individual, inexpensive waffle makers for groups of four (If the program is done with one person demonstrating then serving samples, quantities will be different than when groups at tables are making one of each type of waffle.)
- paper plates
- serving tools such as tongs to remove waffles from the iron
- measuring cups and spoons
- nonstick cooking spray
- plastic cutlery

Brownies
- brownie mix plus items to finish, including possibly canola oil, eggs, vanilla, and water
- extra egg

Pizza
- prepared pizza dough
- pizza sauce
- mozzarella cheese

Baked Apples
- apples (recipe suggests Jonathan), sliced to one-fourth-inch thickness
- sugar

Cornbread
- cornbread mix plus items to finish, including egg, milk, and melted butter

Quesadillas
- tortillas
- shredded cheddar cheese

ACTIVITIES

Set out ingredients for all projects before the program. If groups are making their own, set up ingredients for the same recipe at all four stations. Give an introduction about the waffle-iron trend, showing any library cookbooks about waffles, discussing some websites also, and offering a handout with books and sites listed for reference.

- *Brownies:* The site One Good Thing (www.onegoodthingbyjillee.com/waffle-maker -recipes/) suggests adding one egg to prepared brownie mix before putting it on the waffle iron to bake.

- *Pizza:* Another suggestion from One Good Thing is to put prepared pizza dough right on the waffle iron and cook for two minutes. Then add sauce and mozzarella cheese, holding the iron slightly closed to melt cheese. If families are participating, this would be a good project for adults to supervise.

- *Baked Apples:* As suggested by the Cupcake Project site (www.cupcakeproject .com/one-minute-waffle-iron-baked-apples/), place apple slices on the waffle iron and sprinkle with sugar. Cook for one minute.

- *Cornbread:* Prepare the cornbread mix ahead of the program, or have each table prepare it. Cook as you would a waffle, approximately two minutes or until the light indicator shows that it is done, depending on the waffle maker.

- *Quesadillas:* Put shredded cheddar cheese in between two tortillas and cook on the waffle iron for thirty seconds to one minute, until cheese is melted.

TRIVIA AND OTHER FREE GAMES

- Make a true-or-false list of foods that can be made with a waffle iron on a bookmark with information about the program available.

MARKETING

- Make cards with a faint waffle-looking imprint on one side and a recipe and information about the program on the other.
- A display with a waffle iron surrounded by breakfast or waffle cookbooks will catch attention.

VARIATIONS

- *Waffled:* Offer a contest for creative foods made with waffle makers. Patrons can submit ideas or prepare their entries at the library for a panel of staff or board members to taste. Best savory and sweet recipes can win gift certificates to an area grocery store. All recipes could be published.
- *Holiday Waffles:* After making the investment into waffle makers, use the waffle makers to demonstrate recipes on themes periodically throughout the year, from Thanksgiving leftover updates to quick holiday party appetizers. Some easy recipes may be found here: www.delish.com/cooking/recipe-ideas/g2821/ ways-to-use-waffle-iron/?slide=1.
- *Teen Advisory Board Treats:* If the teen advisory board (TAB) is small (ten or fewer), consider having them make food at meetings—either pizzas or a waffle dessert.

— Middle and High School — Survival Strategies

Growing up is hard to do, and the transition from one school building to another as one advances from elementary school to middle school to high school can be intimidating and a little scary. Give your patrons a chance to destress and get psyched for new adventures with a program that is part informational, part recreational.

PREP TIME	LENGTH OF PROGRAM	NUMBER OF PATRONS	SUGGESTED AGE RANGE
3–4 hours	1 ½ hours	20	Tweens and teens

SUPPLIES/SHOPPING

- snacks
- DIY stress balls
  » standard deflated party balloons
  » rice or flour (or both)
  » funnels
  » scissors
- locker decorations
  » empty mint/candy tins (e.g., Eclipse mints)
  » magnets (from a craft store)
  » E6000 glue
  » Mod Podge
  » old/discarded magazines or comic books
  » paint sponges

ACTIVITIES

- *Advice from Peers*: Set up a panel of current high school students to give advice and information to their incoming peers. Since they've been through middle school as well, they can provide information for incoming junior high students too. You can also have a panel of current middle schoolers to help out the newcomers.

- Highlight resources/programs that the library has that students should take note of (study help, tutors, finals-week study spaces, etc.).

Craft: DIY Stress Ball

1. Stretch out a balloon.
2. Use a funnel to fill the balloon slowly with either flour or rice (be sure to have the table covered no matter which you're using, but rice does make for an easier cleanup). If you are using flour, you'll want to have a pencil handy to use to free up any blockage that occurs as you're filling the balloon.

3. Once the balloon is full (be careful not to pack it full—you want it to still be malleable), tie it closed.
4. Use the scissors to cut off the remaining balloon above the closure.

Craft: Locker Decorations
(inspired by www.themamasgirls.com/diy-magnetic-pen-holder)

1. Glue magnets to the back of a mint container.
2. As the magnets dry, look through magazines/comic books and cut out pieces to collage on the container.
3. Once the magnets have dried, use Mod Podge to affix the pieces to the container.
4. Let dry.

MARKETING

- Reach out to schools to advertise the program in addition to promoting it in your teen and tween areas of the library and on social media.

VARIATIONS

- *Session for Parents:* While their children are attending the previous session(s), have a session for adults that includes tips and information about parenting a middle/high schooler. This will be particularly useful for parents who have their first child entering middle/high school.

PRO TIP

Incorporate elements of the Time Management program in chapter 9 to give patrons a leg up on staying organized when the new school year starts.

Sing-Along Movie Night

Some movie memories just stick with us forever—who doesn't remember singing along to "Greased Lightnin'" or "Hakuna Matata"? Sing along to classic songs that are seared in your memory with a sing-along of a movie or musical for the family. The possibilities for movie choices are unlimited.

PREP TIME	LENGTH OF PROGRAM	NUMBER OF PATRONS	SUGGESTED AGE RANGE
2–3 hours	1 ½ –3 hours, depending on length of movie	40–50	Families

SUPPLIES/SHOPPING

- DVD/Blu-Ray/streaming service of a musical (e.g., *Grease, Mamma Mia, Mary Poppins, Rent, High School Musical*, and *The Sound of Music*)
- Disney movies (e.g., *Beauty and the Beast, The Little Mermaid, Aladdin, The Lion King, Frozen*, and *Moana*)
- large screen for display
- DVD/Blu-Ray player or projection system
- microphone

Popcorn Taste Testing
- variety of popcorn
- popcorn flavor spices
- plastic bowls or popcorn bags
- plastic spoons

Mini Drive-In Movie Theater
- cardboard (saved from technical services)
- markers
- scissors
- masking tape or duct tape (if needed)

ACTIVITIES

- Sing-alongs can work well in many different venues and formats. If your library owns a sing-along version of a popular movie (usually a children's movie), use this version. Alternately, turn on closed captions or subtitles with a regular DVD and let people sing aloud alongside the characters. Set up comfortable chairs or outdoor storytime blankets for patrons to sit on. Dim the lights and start the show!

- Show a movie on a large rental screen outside or project it onto the side of your library. You can create a drive-in experience for the whole family. Block off a section of the parking lot near the site and set your movie to begin at dusk. This is a great after-hours program; it will be beneficial to have fewer people driving through the parking lot. Encourage patrons to bring their own lawn chairs or blankets to enjoy a night outside singing along to favorite movies. Make sure you have a backup rain date or indoor location in case the weather doesn't cooperate.

> **PRO TIP**
>
> Make sure you have the movie rights for the chosen movie(s). Test out the DVD/Blu-Ray and technology one week ahead of time in case there are scratches or other viewing issues.

- Make a mini drive-in theater at the library for younger children. Using large boxes (or a few smaller ones), assemble a small car. Draw on tires and cut out steering wheels from cardboard saved from technical services. Ask your teen advisory board for help with creating the cars and making fun designs on the cars. Younger children have shorter attention spans, so it may be easier to screen a "Best of" Disney songs DVD to sing aloud to the highlights.

- Create a popcorn bar with different flavors of popcorn and spices. Ask patrons to mix and match to discover their perfect combination. Vote on favorites during an intermission and encourage them to try new pairings, such as kettle corn with chili powder or parmesan.

- Hold a movie-themed karaoke program. Encourage your patrons to sing their hearts out to songs in any musical. Use YouTube to find musical clips or song lyrics, hand patrons a microphone, and go! Have patrons write their choice of song and the movie or musical it is in on a sign-in sheet. Staff can create a playlist to help ease transitions from patron to patron. When it's each person's turn to sing, ask them why they chose the song and movie—the answers may surprise you. Allow groups to sign up as well as individuals.

TRIVIA AND OTHER FREE GAMES

- Print song lyrics from the movie and leave one or two words in each verse blank for patrons to fill in with the correct answer.
- Use a word-search generator to create a word search using items specific to the movie, lyrics, characters, and more.
- Match the actor to his or her role in the movie. Print actors' names in one column and their characters' names in another for participants to connect.

MARKETING

- If permitted, use the movie poster or incorporate characters into your promotional materials. Purchase a life-size cardboard cutout of a character and add a word bubble with the program information. Patrons can take pictures with the character and will have a reminder of the program details.

VARIATIONS

- *Teens:* Keep it fresh and exciting with songs from Broadway musicals. It's a great night to celebrate live performances on stage with both recently popular and perennial favorites. Some choice favorites include *Hamilton, Dear Evan Hansen,* and *Phantom of the Opera.*
- *Millennials:* Create an adult-only sing-along and relive childhood memories at this nostalgia-filled program. Any musical movie is a good choice, but this is also a chance to show musicals that hold a special place in millennials' hearts (and that might not be appropriate for a younger audience). Some fun choices include *The Rocky Horror Picture Show, Bohemian Rhapsody, Spamalot,* or *Sweeney Todd.* Alternately, feel free to choose enduring childhood classics, such as *The Lion King, Aladdin,* or *Mary Poppins.* This is a great opportunity to bring adults into the library who do not have children—an elusive age group!

chapter 6

June

LIBRARIES CAN HELP patrons gear up for summer with a combination of fun food and active events. **BBQ for Beginners** helps those who have been afraid to try grilling heat up their food with easy tips for delicious meals. **DIY Frozen Drinks and Desserts** shows tweens, teens, and families how to make easy, crowd-pleasing frozen treats—perfect for hot days. The **Fun Fair** allows libraries to work with teen volunteers on games for intergenerational groups to play in the library—or outdoors. And the **Road Rally/Scavenger Hunt** takes teens outside to find clues and treasure for engaging team fun. There is something for everyone this month.

BBQ for Beginners

Nothing says summer like barbecue fresh off the grill. For inexperienced grillers, the idea of using a grill can be intimidating. Take the confusion away with a demonstration and hands-on grilling program. Fun, educational, and delicious!

PREP TIME	LENGTH OF PROGRAM	NUMBER OF PATRONS	SUGGESTED AGE RANGE
3–4 hours	1 ½ hours	10–20	Millennials

SUPPLIES/SHOPPING

- grill (propane or charcoal)
- tongs
- grill spatula
- grill brush
- wooden skewers
- gallon-size bags
- butter
- oil
- paper plates
- large bowls
- forks
- knives
- napkins

Suggested selections (choose several from each category)

Meat
- ground beef
- chicken
- sirloin steak
- T-bone steak
- sausage
- ribs
- pork

Vegetables and Side Dishes
- corn
- bell peppers
- onion
- zucchini
- mushrooms
- potatoes

Sauces and Seasoning
- salt
- pepper
- steak sauce
- barbecue sauces
- chili powder
- paprika
- onion powder

> **PRO TIP**
>
> Many libraries may require food to be precooked or brought in from a restaurant. Check your library policy before proceeding with this program. Another option is to partner with a local restaurant and host the event off-site.

ACTIVITIES

- Determine the grill basics you would like your patrons to master in this class. These tasks can include grill operation, safety, food prep, and the best temperature to cook each item. If you are not comfortable around a grill, put the call out to library staff to see if they would like to share their knowledge and gain programming experience. Other options include partnering with a local butcher, grocer, or restaurant to have them lead the class.

- Offer an advanced program for seasoned grillmasters or people who have completed the beginner's class. Activities can include creating your own barbecue sauce or marinade, how to use a smoker, and grilling a turkey for Thanksgiving. Include plant-based options for vegetarian burgers.

- Hold a blind burger taste test. Form teams of two or more and allow them ten minutes to prep their burgers however each group sees fit. Make sure each team writes down the ingredients they added, how long they cooked the burger on each side and total time, if the grill lid was closed, and so on. Place one burger from each group on a plate with a number to keep the group anonymous. Ask each person to taste test a piece of each group's burgers and give them a score from one to ten, with ten ranking the highest. After tallying the winner, ask each group to share their process.

- Alternately, hold a blind burger taste-off with restaurants in your community. Reach out to restaurant managers and ask them to bring in hamburger samples for a community tasting. Place restaurant participants' names and logos on marketing materials to highlight their involvement and partnership.

- Expose your patrons to flavors and spices from across the country. Memphis, St. Louis, Texas, and both Carolinas each have their own distinct flavors of barbecue sauce. Taste test and create new meals in this program while discovering the history behind each unique flavor.

MARKETING

- Place flyers in local stores near grills to attract new grill owners. Strategically add flyers in the grilling and cookbook section of the adult nonfiction collection. Create a fun display of grilling utensils, sauce bottles, and grill books in the library.

VARIATIONS

- *Teens:* Many teens will be attending college or living on their own in the near future. While many of them may not have access to a grill, they will need to learn how to cook for themselves—for the first time. Help them get a head start by hosting a class about microwave cooking or cooking for one with a few key meals (spaghetti, baked chicken, pizza, etc.) that can be easily done in a dorm room or apartment. See Life Hacks for Living on Your Own in chapter 8 for inspiration.
- *Older Adults:* Have a recipe swap and ask patrons to bring in their favorite items they cook on the grill. Each person can bring a sample of his or her food and share these creations with others. Everyone will leave with new and tasty recipes to make at home.

DIY Frozen Drinks and Desserts

Summer is the perfect time for frozen drinks and desserts. It can be easy to create crowd-pleasing treats for teens and adults. This program could even work as a family event where members work in small groups to try techniques.

PREP TIME	LENGTH OF PROGRAM	NUMBER OF PATRONS	SUGGESTED AGE RANGE
1 ½ hours	1 hour	25	Tweens, teens, and families (This program can be done with easier or harder techniques and recipes, adjustable for different ages.)

SUPPLIES/SHOPPING

Ice Cream Roses
- tub of vanilla ice cream
- four to five ice cream scoops
- plastic bowls
- spoons

Ice Cream Balls
- vanilla ice cream
- scoops
- coconut
- waxed paper

Ice Cream Sandwiches
- graham crackers, chocolate and regular if possible
- Cool Whip
- Saran wrap

Vanilla Drinks
- 1 c. ice per drink
- 1½ c. milk
- 1½ c. vanilla ice cream
- ¼ tsp. vanilla extract
- ¼ tsp. peppermint flavoring (optional)
- blender
- cups
- straws
- whipped cream (optional)

Chocolate Bananas
- bananas, peeled and frozen
- narrow Popsicle sticks
- fondue pot (or microwave chips to melt)
- milk-chocolate chips
- half-and-half
- sprinkles
- chopped nuts

Strawberry Lemonade Slushies
- lemonade mix
- water
- pitchers
- blender
- ice
- strawberries
- cups
- straws

Easy Sorbet Pie
- premade cookie crust
- ½ gal. sorbet
- ice cream scoop
- sliced strawberries plus blueberries
- knife plus spatula to serve
- optional: waffle bowls or cones

ACTIVITIES

Choose three of the desserts to make with the group. For families, purchase enough supplies so four times as many treats can be made. Or choose some to demonstrate and serve small portions of, such as the slushy.

Everyone should leave with supply lists and recipes.

> **PRO TIP**
>
> Invite strong teens to help with scooping. Invite teen volunteers to help with this one, including setup and cleanup, in exchange for treats.

- *Rose Scoops:* Put a scoop of ice cream in front of each person, in the waffle bowls or plastic bowls. Everyone can use the scoop to press into the ball of ice cream to make a rose design.

- *Ice Cream Balls:* Put wax paper in front of everyone. Have them sprinkle coconut on the waxed paper, and put a scoop of ice cream in the center. Everyone can use his or her hands or spoons to roll the ice cream ball in the coconut before eating. Discuss ideas for other things that ice cream could be rolled in, including nuts or graham cracker/ cookie crumbs.

- *Ice Cream Sandwiches:* If a freezer is available at the library, have class members put Cool Whip between two layers of graham crackers, then wrap gently in Saran. Use Sharpies to add names. Put sandwiches in the freezer. They can take and eat them at the end of the hour.

- *Vanilla Drinks:* Similar to those from a popular coffee chain, these are part shake, part smoothie. Blend all ingredients except whipped cream and pour into drinks. Add whipped cream.

- *Frozen Bananas:* Put milk-chocolate chips and half-and-half into the fondue pot (or melt the chips in a microwave). Have class members dip frozen bananas (with Popsicle sticks inserted in one end) in the chocolate before drying on waxed paper. Everyone can add sprinkles or nuts to each. Let dry and eat.

- *Strawberry Lemonade Slushies:* Make one serving of lemonade with the mix and water (multiple servings if demonstrating for an entire group). Blend ice with cut strawberries in the blender. Add the lemonade mixture until desired thickness.

- *Easy Sorbet Pie:* Allow the sorbet to soften a bit prior to trying this recipe. Then have members of the group help scoop it into the pie shell, making it into a smooth pie. Add toppings.

TRIVIA AND OTHER FREE GAMES

- Vote on favorite Popsicle or frozen treats online or with a voting box near the teen area, decorated with pictures of frozen treats. Have teen advisory board members make the box, and choose some favorite treats to have on ballots. The voting could also take place through a survey on Twitter or on the library website. Near the voting area, recipes and information about the course should be handy on a flyer or in a link.

MARKETING

- Food programs rarely need lots of marketing. Colorful signs or posters with frozen treats pictured will help.
- A display of treats with sundae glasses and scoops will also attract attention.

VARIATIONS

- *Millennials:* Millennials may enjoy making the vanilla drinks and ice cream pies, along with more variations, including frozen yogurt parfaits.
- *Older Adults:* Older adults may enjoy a program on the history of ice cream, sodas, and sundaes, an overview of popular treats and recipes from decades past. This information can be found at www.foodtimeline.org. They could eat prepared frozen treats during the program.

Fun Fair

Celebrate a fun afternoon of games at the library. People of all ages will enjoy spending the day at the library (or newly minted boardwalk) learning new games, participating in contests, and earning prizes. Games offer a host of new skills for children, young and old, such as cooperative game play, patience, competition, and learning how to follow rules. Hosting a fun fair is a great way to get all ages involved at the library: tweens and teens can help build life-size games, millennials and older adults can bring young children to the fair, and it's a great opportunity to reach out to local schools to borrow midway games and cut down on costs. Celebrating gaming is a great intergenerational program that all ages can appreciate.

PREP TIME	LENGTH OF PROGRAM	NUMBER OF PATRONS	SUGGESTED AGE RANGE
12–15 hours	2–3 hours	Unlimited, if your library can reasonably accommodate	Families

SUPPLIES/SHOPPING

- star stickers
- boardwalk card
- sidewalk chalk
- table
- chairs (two)

Candyland Supplies
- interlocking foam squares (variety of colors) or laminated construction paper
- Candyland character cutouts (large)
- Candyland spinners (three to four if possible)
- plastic balls
- cellophane wrap
- cardstock
- PVC pipe
- scissors
- ribbon
- markers

Guess Who? Supplies
- foam-core board
- character prints
- glue
- scissors
- PVC pipe

Boardwalk Games (Examples)
- Skee-Ball
- Bozo buckets
- ring toss
- bean-bag toss

Contest Supplies
- stopwatch
- Hula-Hoops (Hula-Hoop contest)
- water bottles (bottle-flipping contest)
- bandanas (three-legged race)
- eggs, hard-boiled (egg race)
- plastic spoons (egg race)
- dunk tank rental (if possible)
- prizes (variety of small games and toys)

ACTIVITIES, CRAFTS, TRIVIA, AND OTHER FREE GAMES

Begin planning your fun fair and assess the space you have, games you want to include, and what games can be created (ideally by your teen advisory board or volunteers). Create an area for boardwalk games, contests, and life-size games. Use the sidewalk to create individual masterpieces of chalk art. Prepare for the possibility of inclement weather and have indoor space options as a backup. Purchase bulk toy assortment prizes to give away as prizes.

- Create an activity card (similar to a Bingo card) to pass out to all attendees, with each game or contest listed in a different square. After participating in a contest or game, each person will get a sticker to mark that he or she did the activity. Once he or she finishes the card (or gets a certain number or pattern), they get a prize. This will encourage patrons to explore the fun fair and try new games and activities and make the lines flow smoothly. Include information about the location of the prize table and the times and locations of the contests on the card. Set up a prize table or booth for kids to choose a prize from a treasure chest after they complete their card. Mark cards that have received prizes with a unique designated sticker.

- Ask your teen advisory board what board games they would like to help transform into life-sized games; Candyland and Guess Who? are two simple possibilities. Create Guess Who? with characters voted by teens, encourage them to think outside the box, and use characters from books, movies, comics, or pop culture. Once fifteen to twenty characters are chosen, enlarge and print them for teens to cut and glue each picture (twice) to a large 2 × 3 ft. foam-core board. Add a giant question mark on the back of each board with two different colors for the same character to denote his or her side. Attach character boards to individual PVC pipes and line them up in rows to create a Guess Who? grid.

- Create a Candyland pathway by interlocking colorful foam squares into a path (alternately, construction paper taped to the floor will work as well, but laminate it to prevent it from being ripped and destroyed). If possible, purchase Candyland stand-up characters and settings such as the Candy Castle or Peppermint Forest. Alternately, the teen advisory board can develop creative ways to make it feel like Candyland, such as creating a bag of gobstoppers from playgroup balls, creating large lollipops out of PVC pipe and cardstock, or using large candy-cane decorations to create the Peppermint Forest. Participants in life-size Candyland can go as groups or singles, and multiple groups can go at intervals, as long as there is more than one spinner.

- Determine what contests would be easy and accessible to host at the fun fair. Think of games that are easily done without a lot of supplies or mess, especially if you need to hold your event indoors. Some simple ideas include
  - » Hula-Hoop contest
  - » three-legged race
  - » water-bottle-flipping contest
  - » egg relay race

- Have the same contest twice in a row with different age groups, one for younger children eight and under and one for older children and teens so they can compete fairly among peers. Encourage your TAB group to help run or monitor the games and contests on the day of the fun fair.

- Choose your fun fair's boardwalk games. These can include Skee-Ball, Bozo buckets, a bean-bag toss, a ring toss, and so on. If your library has any of these games (or others that are similar), include them in your fair. If your library does not own many boardwalk-esque games, reach out to schools or park districts in your area. Many schools or community groups host their own fun fairs throughout the school year, and ask to borrow a few boardwalk games.

- Amp up your fun fair with a rental of a dunk tank and balloon artists, if the budget permits. Having a dunk tank is a lighthearted moment to have fun with your community and staff. Ask your library director and government officials to participate. And, of course, if you want to get in the dunk tank, go for it! Make sure you have a rotation of participants—any longer than twenty to thirty minutes in the seat is tiring and leaves participants waterlogged.

- Ask for staff volunteers to help run individual events at the fun fair. You can't be in a million different places at once running each game, event, and contest, so reaching out to staff, library volunteers, and TAB members is critical. Prepare instructions for each game, and also give each person the answers to basic FAQs about where prizes, other games, and contests are located.

MARKETING

- Place a boardwalk game in your lobby a few weeks before the fun fair and encourage participants to play. Hang a poster or have flyers near the game that advertise the fun fair with multiple games and contests.
- If your library circulates or has games in house, create fun fair flyers and hand them out with a board-game checkout. Make sure to include pictures or graphics of games and activities that will be available that day.

VARIATIONS

- Consider having an indoor winter fun fair. Break up the winter blues by hosting a fun fair inside your library during the cold winter months. Most of these program ideas can easily be done indoors as long as space is available. Switch sidewalk chalk to a craft indoors, such as drawing on black construction paper with chalk or iridescent markers or pens.

Road Rally/
Scavenger Hunt

Take scavenger hunts out of the regular confines of the library and into your community. Create clues and checkpoints for teams to reach and earn points. Teams must stick together, document their route, and solve clues set by library staff. Cap it all off with an ice cream bar to celebrate the attendees' sleuthing skills.

PREP TIME	LENGTH OF PROGRAM	NUMBER OF PATRONS	SUGGESTED AGE RANGE
4–6 hours	1 ½ hours	Unlimited	Teens

SUPPLIES/SHOPPING

- golf pencils
- clipboard for each team
- tokens for clues
- stopwatch
- ice cream
- ice cream scoop
- paper bowls
- plastic spoons
- napkins
- variety of ice cream toppings

ACTIVITIES, TRIVIA, AND OTHER FREE GAMES

- Design a scavenger hunt that takes place in and around the library. Make sure you have at least two to three staff members; one or two outside to monitor the teams in case there are any problems and one staff person inside to set up the ice cream bar and be in the program room for any early returnees. Scavenger hunt clues can include finding the specials of the day at a local ice cream shop, the name of the dentist in the local practice, the name of a book in a display case, or the price of a candy bar at the grocery store, and so on. Include checkpoints for teams to find a staff member and have them write a symbol for the answer or take a picture with the staff member. Have this be more than just a stopping point; make the teams do a goofy challenge such as ten jumping jacks before they can get their checkpoint symbol. Ask local businesses to participate, especially if groups of people will be entering their places of business. Create the same scavenger hunt for everyone, but switch the starting points for each team so they don't run into each other. Each team gets one road rally/scavenger hunt paper and can pick their team name.

- Make sure each patron is part of a team, and set a time when teams must all be back in the program room, approximately one hour after the program begins. Have each team set an alarm on a phone five minutes before they need to return to the program room. Encourage teams to walk, stick together, and do the scavenger hunt in order to avoid running into other teams. Amp up your scavenger hunt by having groups take a photo of each answer or checking in with a group photo at certain points. Use the time when teens are looking for clues to set up the ice cream bar. Once teens come in, allow them to go through the ice cream bar, and staff can begin grading the answer sheets. The team with the most correct answers wins.

- Theme your Road Rally to match your summer reading theme. Use symbols associated with the theme, such as music notes for a musical theme, and use them as clues or symbols to find and take a picture with.

- Create an online scavenger hunt that teens can do in the program or as a passive program online. On the top of the sheet is a list of twenty-six different types of websites that can be found on the Internet (examples: sport, insurance company, education, department store, etc.). Each team must find a website that is on each of those topics. Each site has to start with a different letter of the alphabet. You cannot use Aflac for insurance and Alabama State University for education because they both begin with the letter A. Source: http://scavenger -hunt.org/wp-content/uploads/2013/11/Internet -Scavenger-Hunt-Worksheet.pdf.

> **PRO TIP**
>
> Make a backup version that takes place inside in case of inclement weather. Inform library staff so they are not concerned when groups of teens or adults are scavenging for clues throughout the stacks.

MARKETING

- Design a flyer with symbols of a road rally or scavenger hunt: maps, a checkered flag, and so on. Advertise with local businesses if they are participating or in car repair shops.

VARIATIONS

- *Passive Program:* Create a passive program for teams to complete over the course of a few weeks by car. This gives the library more flexibility with staff and a chance for participants to explore the community more in depth. Ask businesses to participate or put the call out online. Create an online Q&A form and have teams submit their answers and checkpoint pictures. Each team will GPS track their route and submit a screenshot of it and the time it took to complete the course to the library staff in charge of the program.

chapter 7

July

FAMILY FUN IS the theme for several program ideas this month. Bring back crafts and more with **Camp Nostalgia** as families create memories together. A library **Spelling Bee** adds new twists to the popular trend for tweens or families. Invite talented young people to show their skill! Too often families today don't have time to enjoy a **Night under the Stars**, but the library is ready to help them do it with spectacular sky gazing. And the programs for this month end with a **Wonderful Wedding Series** for millennials and older adults that covers traditions from years ago and today as well as featuring wedding styles from across the globe.

Camp Nostalgia

Hearken back to simpler times with a fun, casual program filled with the activities from summer days past.

PREP TIME	LENGTH OF PROGRAM	NUMBER OF PATRONS	SUGGESTED AGE RANGE
2–3 hours	2 hours	20–25	Millennials and older adults (great family program)

SUPPLIES/SHOPPING

- embroidery thread (various colors)
- clothespins
- plastic cording
- lanyard hooks
- coloring books
- crayons/colored pencils/markers
- board games (checkers, Sorry!, Candyland)
- decks of cards
- cups
- graham crackers
- marshmallows (Marshmallow Fluff if no access to micro-wave/bonfire)
- chocolate bars (chocolate frosting/cookie spread if no access to microwave/bonfire)
- empty Pringles cans with lids (cleaned/wiped out as best as possible)
- empty sardine cans (or similarly sized cans)
- X-Acto knife

ACTIVITIES AND CRAFTS

- Present attendees with various options to choose from at this program. Have stations for crafts, games, and snacks!

- Consider holding this program outside at a local park or on the grounds of your library if you've got the space, but be sure to have an alternate inside location in the event of inclement weather.

- *S'mores:* If you don't have access to a microwave (if your program is taking place inside) or a bonfire (if you're able to pair with a local park district), use marshmallow fluff and chocolate frosting/cookie spread to make indoor s'mores!

- *Friendship Bracelet Craft:* There are infinite ways to braid and weave friendship bracelets. For simple instructions, consult www.instructables.com/id/how-to-make-a-friendship-bracelet-1.

- *Boondoggle Keychain Craft:* For simple instructions in making boondoggle keychains, consult www.instructables.com/id/Engl-3100-Boondoggle.

- *Pringles-Can Bird Feeder Craft:* Use the X-Acto knife to cut one opening in the bottom of the can to fit the sardine can. Slide the sardine can in, making sure it fits snugly. Remove the lid and pour in birdseed.

TRIVIA AND OTHER FREE GAMES

- Your library likely has some if not all the board games mentioned earlier, which is a great way to provide options without having to incur costs. If you're feeling ambitious, you could have a lightning game of trivia and include questions about movies, TV shows, books, and so on that take place at summer camp.

MARKETING

- Create a display of movies that take place at summer camp (*The Parent Trap*, *Wet Hot American Summer*, *Meatballs*, *Ernest Goes to Camp*, etc.) and include information about the program.

VARIATIONS

- *Library Day Camp:* The same basic program can be facilitated for tweens/teens as well, though it would require potentially more structured craft/games segments (i.e., begin a group game or two before moving on to a craft).

Night under the Stars

From eclipses to blood moons, there is always something happening in our solar system. Gazing at the stars has been a popular pastime, and now is the perfect time to share exciting adventures happening in the skies. Pique your patrons' interests with a night under the stars and exciting space-themed activities.

PREP TIME	LENGTH OF PROGRAM	NUMBER OF PATRONS	SUGGESTED AGE RANGE
3–4 hours	1 hour, unless waiting for a celestial event	20–30	Tweens and families

SUPPLIES/SHOPPING

Star Map
- paper
- pencils
- plastic glow-in-the-dark stars
- Sharpie
- tape

Pinhole Camera
- cardstock (or note cards)
- foil
- tape
- paper clip or pin

Rocket Launch
- paper, colored or printer
- plastic 35 mm film canister
- scissors
- tape
- colored pencils, crayons, or markers
- antacid tablets (one per rocket launch)
- water
- eye protection

ACTIVITIES AND CRAFTS

- Have a star party! Plan this around exciting astronomical events happening in your area. If there is a community telescope in your area, consider reaching out to them to partner on a stargazing party. If you live in a more rural area and have the opportunity to see the stars from your library, reach out to the administration to see if you could hold the star party on the roof of the library. Alternatively, seek out your local astronomy society or planetarium and see if they will teach a class about how to use a telescope, identifying stars, or fascinating facts about the solar system. Reach out to local community centers, museums, and colleges and see if they would be willing to teach or host a program in partnership with the library. People of all ages will be excited to attend this event.

- Teach tweens how to navigate the solar system based on a paper-sky version of the orientation of the stars, often called a star chart. Use StarDome (www .astronomy.com/stardome) to orient the stars according to your location. Before the program begins, affix plastic glow-in-the-dark stars to the ceiling and then give tweens the task of identifying which stars make up constellations. Number the stars with black Sharpie markers so students can say which numbers make up specific constellations. Test them before the program and at the end so they can see their progress.

- Plan a solar eclipse viewing party (coincide this with the day of the solar eclipse) and make pinhole cameras using cardstock (or note cards), foil, and tape. Cut a 3 × 3″ square in the center of a piece of cardstock paper. Cover the hole with a piece of foil and secure it with tape. Make a tiny hole in the foil using a pin or paper clip. Place the second piece of cardstock on the ground and hold the piece with aluminum foil above it with the foil facing up. Make sure the sun is behind you to view the projected image on the cardstock on the ground. The farther away you hold your camera, the bigger the projected image will be.

- Use a paper plate to create a sundial that tells time by the power of the sun. Print clock faces that will fit on the back of a paper plate. Paint or color the back edges of the plate or leave it plain. Cut out the clock face and glue it on the back of the plate. Punch a hole in the center of the plate using a pencil. The pencil shadow will help determine the time. Secure it and head outdoors. Position the sundial with the "12" pointing north.

- Build and launch your own rocket. NASA Space Place provides a great innovative way to safely launch a homemade rocket—with bubbles! An outdoor open space is required for this program. Wrap and tape a tube of paper around a film canister with the lid end of the canister down. Add fins to the rocket body (if you choose to) and create a nose cone to tape to the top of the rocket. Decorate your rocket with markers, stickers, crayons, and so on. Go outside for launch. Put on eye protection and fill the canister one-third full of water. Drop an antacid tablet into the canister and snap the lid tightly on. Place the rocket on the ground, stand back, and wait for launch. Ask teams to identify what makes the different rockets soar higher or longer. If there is time, teams can make adjustments to their rockets to test out their theories. Make sure you find all rockets before finishing the program. Source: https://spaceplace.nasa.gov/pop-rocket/en/.

TRIVIA AND OTHER FREE GAMES

- Theme a trivia night entirely around space and science. Questions can include planetary science, visuals of planets to identify, and interesting facts about the space race or astronauts. Another option is to include science-fiction questions as well, such as trivia about *Star Wars*, *Guardians of the Galaxy*, *Ender's Game*, or *Star Trek*. Offer astronaut ice cream as a prize for the winning team.

MARKETING

- Create an interactive display and challenge patrons to put the planets in the solar system in the correct order. Paint or color Styrofoam balls and label each with one of the planet names: Mercury, Venus, Earth, Mars, Jupiter, Saturn, Neptune, and Uranus. Library staff may or may not choose to include Pluto (depending on scientific research at the time of the program). This can also be done as an online challenge or a game in a science-themed program.

VARIATIONS

- *Families:* Check out the website Story Time from Space and watch an astronaut tell a space-themed story from space. Source: storytimefromspace.com. Story Time from Space also provides a great selection of space-themed stories and educational videos. If you are unable to screen a story from space, have an Out of This World space-themed story time. Some popular space books: *Mousetronaut Goes to Mars* by astronaut Mark Kelly, *How to Catch a Star* by Oliver Jeffers, and *Penguinaut!* by Marcie Colleen. Don't forget to sing Laurie Berkner's "Rocketship Run" or "Twinkle, Twinkle, Little Star."
- Learn about life as an astronaut, the education and training needed, upcoming missions, and what it's like to be in the space program. NASA takes requests and coordinates visits for astronauts at high schools and universities, community organizations, businesses and associations, and military organizations. Presentations can be done virtually or in person. Request an appearance at www.nasa .gov/about/speakers/astronautappearances.html.
- *Teens:* Does your library have Lego Mindstorms EV3s? Challenge your teens to rescue the Mars Rover using your Mindstorms. Teens will have to create a series of maneuvers by coding their Mindstorms. See the Lego education website for more details: education.lego.com/en-us/downloads/mindstorms-ev3/curriculum.
- *Older Adults:* Screen any number of space-themed movies, from dramatizations of real events such as *Apollo 13*, *Hidden Figures*, and *First Man*, to documentaries such as *Apollo 11*. Hold a discussion after the movie.

Spelling Bee

Many of us have fond—or perhaps not-so-fond—memories of the school spelling bee. Holding a spelling bee at your library can be a great enhancement to your summer reading program for younger patrons and families or a fun trip down memory lane for millennial patrons.

PREP TIME	LENGTH OF PROGRAM	NUMBER OF PATRONS	SUGGESTED AGE RANGE
3–4 hours	1 ½ hours (potentially longer depending on how you structure it)	10 contestants + audience members	All ages (great family program)

SUPPLIES/SHOPPING
- microphones
- laptop

ACTIVITIES
- Search for lists of commonly misspelled words in order to start compiling the words for your bee. If you are holding the bee for different age levels (tweens and teens, for example), you can also search for lists of words frequently used in school spelling bees/spelling tests. If your spelling bee is part of your summer reading challenge, consider using words that are related to the theme. If you're holding the bee for millennials, consider including buzzwords from past eras that have since fallen out of regular usage (tubular, gnarly, righteous, grody, and bodacious).

VARIATIONS
- *Family Feud!*: Get the whole family involved by running the bee family feud–style. Have two families with the same amount of members play against each other. There are a couple of options for structuring this: (1) the first person gets a word that they have to spell in its entirety, or (2) you start the word with the first person who begins with the first letter and then move down the line, and each subsequent member has to provide the next letter.
- *Dictionary Bee*: Instead of having a spelling bee, consider having a dictionary bee in which contestants are required to define the words instead of spelling them.

PRO TIP

More than one staff member will be required to run this program efficiently and effectively! Consider having one person to read the words to contestants and provide subsequent information (part of speech, language of origin, etc.) and another staff person to get contestants registered and maintain the order.

Keep your list of words on a laptop/tablet with each word hyperlinked to the dictionary entry for easy access to all the subsequent information (part of speech, definition, etc.) rather than creating a cumbersome Word document.

— Wonderful Wedding Series —

Part history, part tips, this series of events will show audience members fun traditions, past and present, and those from countries all over the world.

PREP TIME	LENGTH OF PROGRAM	NUMBER OF PATRONS	SUGGESTED AGE RANGE
2 hours per session	1 hour per session	30	Millennials and older adults

SUPPLIES/SHOPPING

- small cakes or cupcakes (optional)
- tea and coffee
- bottled water
- sparkling grape juice (optional)
- plates
- cups for hot drinks

ACTIVITIES

This program is a series of wedding-themed events.

- *Vintage Weddings and Showers:* This one may appeal mostly to older adults, as it will cover past traditions for themed showers, bridesmaid luncheons, and wedding fashions. This presentation can be put together by library staff to include photos of famous wedding attire or wedding cakes for an enjoyable trip down the memory lane of past bridal styles and traditions. A fashion, history, or culinary professional may be another person to speak on some of these themes for a fun historical program.

- *Modern Wedding Twists:* Aimed at millennials, this program will feature techniques for some modern wedding traditions in the United States.

  » *How to Become Ordained Online and Officiate at a Wedding:* This will include places to find quotes, options for vows, and how to conduct ceremonies and wedding rehearsals.
  » *Oathing Stones:* This may appeal to those who do not wish to have weddings with a religious service.
  » *Jumping the Broom:* Show modern versions of jumping the broom, including how brooms are decorated for the special day for African American weddings.
  » *Easy Wedding Crafts:* Ask professionals or staff from craft stores to show fast and easy ways to make ring-bearer pillows, garters, and even simple headpieces. If there is a lot of interest in these crafts, they could be moved to a separate event.

» *International Wedding Traditions*: Ask members of local international clubs to help staff find professionals who can do brief demonstrations of Indian dancing for weddings, show Mendi painting, and display Indian wedding attire, saris, and jewelry. Other international demonstrations could highlight Asian and Mexican wedding traditions, including clothing and tea ceremonies for Asian traditions and coins and the Lazo rosary for Mexican traditions.

» Groups in the area may be available for different ethnicities and heritages, and getting more varied wedding traditions is optimal for this series. The international traditions could be demonstrated over several programs.

TRIVIA AND OTHER FREE GAMES

• *Match the Tradition to the Country:* To build interest, make a simple quiz matching traditions to the country or region. Draw from those who enter or participate online for a gift certificate to a bakery or restaurant.

MARKETING

• Make a display or an electronic slide show showing the different traditions that will be discussed at the different sessions.

chapter 8

August

AUGUST IS TRANSITION time for many people with the start of a new season and a new school year. **Life Hacks for Living on Your Own** helps older teens and millennials learn valuable skills to make life easier in dorms, apartments, or homes. **Résumé/Cover Writing (When You Don't Have a Long Job History)** helps those applying for jobs describe the skills needed to make lasting impressions. A **Superheroes IRL** event offers all ages a break with a family event delving into the history of favorite characters. And **Tabletop Game Night** offers another type of interactive family fun with traditional and new games to enjoy.

Life Hacks for
Living on Your Own

The transition from living with your family to living alone can be a difficult and confusing process. Help your patrons learn some tips and tricks and bypass some common pitfalls they may encounter as they enter a new phase in their lives. Adulting is challenging; let's give patrons some helpful skills as they navigate the real world.

PREP TIME	LENGTH OF PROGRAM	NUMBER OF PATRONS	SUGGESTED AGE RANGE
3 hours	1 hour	20–30	Older teens, millennials

SUPPLIES/SHOPPING

Budget Supplies
- computers/laptops
- alternatives: preprinted budget template, paper, and pencil

Cooking for One
- measuring cups or spoons
- items to measure: flour, sugar, and so on
- hand sanitizer or sink and water
- paper towels
- chosen meal items

Sewing Basics
- sewing needles
- thread
- scissors
- fabric or clothes
- buttons

Fix-It Challenges
- rubber bands
- vinegar
- water
- cardboard or kitty litter
- red-herring items of choice

Supermarket Challenge
- library baskets
- variety of grocery items: cereal, milk, coffee grounds, toilet paper, and so on
- Alternate options: find plastic toy food or create cardboard cutouts in the shape of each food and labelled appropriately.

ACTIVITIES, CRAFTS, TRIVIA, AND OTHER FREE GAMES

- Ask patrons to divide up a prospective entry-level salary and discuss how they would spend their money. Create a choose-your-own-adventure scenario for patrons. Offer opportunities such as different levels of housing, cars, or distance from work. Based off of their choices, what would the effect be on their lives? Make this an interactive presentation and ask patrons to explain their decisions and what their effects would be, both short and long-term. Budget websites and templates can be found online to use (Google Drive, Mint, Microsoft Office, etc.), or you could print out a salary template to use with paper and pencils. Another option is to have patrons draw at random from a hat for their job, salary, and housing. Create a category of unexpected life expenses such as car repair, an out-of-town wedding, medical bills, taxes, and so on that patrons draw from once or twice. Have each patron work through the unexpected expenses and determine how they would make ends meet.

- Some people may have little to no experience with cooking for themselves or their family or may only know how to cook for a family of three or more. Help ease their transition to single living and teach how to cook for one person. Introduce basics such as proper food handling, how to evenly measure items, the beginnings of meal preparation, meals that last for more than three days, and some go-to entrées that are simple and delicious. Check out http://singly scrumptious.com and https://onedishkitchen.com for inspiration. Print out or send an e-mail of the entrées prepared so your patrons have a handy reference.

- Does anybody have a rip or missing button on his or her favorite clothing item? Don't throw it away; fix it. Teach the basics of sewing and repairing clothing with a simple hand-sewing needle and thread. Start at the beginning and have patrons thread the needle and knot it. This practice is harder than it looks, and some patrons may have never used a needle and thread before. Once attendees can successfully thread a needle, move on to sewing a straight line on a piece of fabric. Once they have started to get the hang of sewing, encourage them to make smaller stitches. Cut tears into the sample fabric or donated clothing and allow patrons to stitch them up cleanly. Don't forget how to demonstrate how to tie-off a knot and to mention that it should be knotted at least three times. Show hints to sewing a button and repairing a torn shirt (double your thread for button sewing and leave space when sewing so it isn't pulled taut when a piece of fabric gets between the button and the clothing you're sewing). If you have advanced sewers, give them slightly more difficult tasks, such as hemming a pair of pants. Ask your colleagues if anyone has any particular sewing skills and is interested in helping if you are not comfortable leading this program.

- Set up problem-solving challenges for each patron to complete that may come up in everyday life. For example, a lid is stuck on a jar and cannot be opened. Look around the room—what can you do to open the jar, and what everyday items can be used? (Wrap rubber bands around the lid of the jar.) You need to clean the bathroom but don't have any cleaning products; what can you use? (Try vinegar and water.) Your car gets stuck in the snow with the wheels spinning; how can you get traction to leave your parking spot? (Lay kitty litter or cardboard under the tires.) You have a job interview in one hour, but your go-to interview shirt is wrinkled and you don't own an iron; how do you get out the wrinkles? (Leave it in the bathroom with the shower on so the steam takes them out.) This can be done by explaining the various situations with no visuals or providing the props to complete these challenges, with some items as red herrings, of course. You never know what patrons are going to come up with; hearing their hacks and how-tos is a great learning opportunity for everyone.

- Have a *Supermarket Sweep* or *Price Is Right* contest. This will help patrons assess the value of many common household items and help them form a grocery budget. Items can include laundry detergent, a gallon of milk, chips, vegetables, and so on. If you play the *Price Is Right*, ask patrons (three at a time) the cost of an item, and the person with the closest price (without going over) wins. Keep playing until you have finalists and then a winner! Offer the winner—or finalists—one of the grocery items as a prize, if the budget allows for it. For *Supermarket Sweep*, set out various grocery items and give the contestants a budget they have to stick to (and also eat for few days) and items to gather within a set time limit, usually around one minute, thirty seconds. Use library baskets for patrons to carry their items. Alternatively, use plastic toy food items (borrowed from youth services) or create cardboard cutouts of grocery items. Research food prices before the program or have your receipt handy.

- Hold a presentation about first-time renting and what to expect when you sign a lease. Determine what the responsibilities are for the tenant and owner. Does the renter buy and install air filters? If there is a flood, does the owner pay for alternate housing until everything is cleaned? Invite a local lawyer or apartment leasing company representative and discuss tenant rights, the importance of reading a contract, hidden clauses, and deposits.

MARKETING

- Don't forget to advertise how the library can help those setting out on their own. Maybe your library has a welcome gift basket for newcomers to the area. Advertise the value of the library card: books, online resources, DVDs, exciting programs, and of course, Wi-Fi.

VARIATIONS

- *Tweens:* Create meals or snacks in a jar using basic ingredients and a mason jar. These can be as simple as vegetable sticks; a variety of fruit, crackers, and cheese; or yogurt and granola. Offer an assortment of ingredients (fruits, vegetables, yogurt, pretzels, etc.) and encourage patrons to try different combinations.
- Create microwave mug treats—no stove or oven required. Provide the microwave, mugs, spoons, ingredients, and a few recipes to try. Recipes can include chocolate-chip cookies, cinnamon rolls, eggs, pizza, and more.
- *Teens:* Ask college freshmen in your community to speak to high school teens about dorm life or their first year of college—the expectations versus reality. If you are in contact with former teen advisory board members who have gone to college, reach out to them or talk to student affairs at a local college to see if any students would be willing to speak about their experiences and what they wished they knew before going to college.

Résumé / Cover Letter Writing
(When You Don't Have a Long Job History)

A fundamental skill to acquire before entering the workforce is writing a résumé and a cover letter. However, due to a variety of factors (limited or solitary job experience, lack of resources), opportunities to improve upon or even get a start on this skill are always in demand.

PREP TIME	LENGTH OF PROGRAM	NUMBER OF PATRONS	SUGGESTED AGE RANGE
1–2 hours	1 hour	20	Teens

SUPPLIES/SHOPPING

- pens/pencils/paper for attendees to take notes
- computer/presentation screen

ACTIVITIES

- Consider presenting this program with the librarian on staff whose primary responsibility is job resources. They can provide valuable insight for your patrons as well and are familiar with providing résumé/cover letter assistance.

- Highlight any resources/databases your library has that provide help in preparing résumés and cover letters, in addition to having on hand several of the print books/guides in the collection.

- After you have gone over the basic components of a résumé and how to structure it (it is particularly helpful to have a résumé template up on screen as a visual aid), ask attendees to write down anything they are involved in—activities/clubs at school, volunteering, babysitting/lawn care, community events with which they've helped out, church involvement, and so on. After they have done this, have them write down next to each one what skills/values they learned at each role. Give them some examples to help get started: playing sports helped them learn teamwork and communication, working at Target helped them learn punctuality and customer service, and so on. Explain the importance of recognizing/highlighting the value of the experiences they have had and how they have helped prepare them for the workforce.

- In addition to going over the format and structure of a résumé/cover letter, a key element of this program is showing these teens how to highlight the fun-

> **PRO TIP**
>
> Pair this program with a version of the Toastmasters/TED Talks/Public Speaking program in chapter 11 to practice interviewing skills!

damental skills they have acquired from the various activities they have participated in already and use that to bolster their résumé—limited job experience notwithstanding.

MARKETING

- Reach out to local high schools and let them know the details of the program so that they can share the information with students. Don't forget to advertise on social media too!
- Create a display of the résumé and cover letter writing materials that your library has available to promote the program for adults listed under variations.

VARIATIONS

- *Adults Coming Back to the Workforce:* A similar program can be offered for adults who are reentering the job force after some time away for any number of reasons (parents who have taken time away from work to raise children, for example). Entering the job market is intimidating no matter what age a person is, but it can be especially so for adults who feel out of touch with the current workforce.

Superheroes IRL

Who were the men and women behind the superhero—both the creators and the inspirations? This program delves into the stories behind some of the most familiar faces in our current pop culture landscape and will leave patrons with a new appreciation for the often underrated medium of comics as well as the superheroes in their lives.

PREP TIME	LENGTH OF PROGRAM	NUMBER OF PATRONS	SUGGESTED AGE RANGE
3–4 hours	1 hour	20–25	All ages (great for families)

SUPPLIES/SHOPPING

- There are no supplies necessary for this program, but consider having the items from your collection mentioned under "Marketing" so that patrons can have examples in addition to any visual aids a presenter may bring.

ACTIVITIES

- Partner with someone in your community who is knowledgeable about the history of comics and comics creators (someone from your local comic shop, an instructor at a local college or university, or perhaps someone on the library staff) to present the information in this program.
- For additional engagement with your patrons, ask them to list (they don't have to share unless they want to) a person they know in real life who they would use as inspiration for creating a superhero and why.

TRIVIA AND OTHER FREE GAMES

- There is no shortage of trivia that can be asked about comics—particularly, the history of comics. Consider peppering in some trivia questions whose answers will be surprising and worthy of additional explanation by your presenter.

MARKETING

- Create a display of comic books and graphic novels whose contributors include the individuals who will be discussed at the program, as well as nonfiction materials about those creators or about the history of the medium itself, and include on it information about the program.

VARIATIONS

- *Tweens and Teens:* Take the topic at hand in another direction and invite to the library some IRL superheroes to present a look at what it takes to perform certain jobs that keep your community running (e.g., health care professionals, police officers, park district employees, and social workers).

Tabletop Game Night

For the family or individual(s) looking to escape screen time and engage in IRL socializing, a tabletop game night is a fun and engaging (not to mention free!) option. Participants can enjoy playing some classic games as well as learning about new ones!

PREP TIME	LENGTH OF PROGRAM	NUMBER OF PATRONS	SUGGESTED AGE RANGE
2 hours	3 hours (structured as a drop-in)	Dependent on the number of games available	All ages (great family program)

SUPPLIES/SHOPPING

- tabletop games for a variety of ages and playing levels
  - » Suggestions: Monopoly, Life, Stratego, Checkers, Chess, Sorry, Trouble, decks of cards, Labyrinth, Apples to Apples, Exploding Kittens, Chutes and Ladders, and more
- snacks

ACTIVITIES

- Set up your program area with several tables for gaming. As this program is open to all ages, make sure you have games at varying difficulty levels and playing ability available for participants to choose from.

MARKETING

- Market this program in all spaces of your library, including the youth department, teen department, and adult department. An additional option is to market it in your AV department with a polite sign imploring patrons to give up a little bit of screen time for some good old-fashioned board games.

VARIATIONS

- *Tabletop Tournament*: Rather than structuring this program as a free-for-all, set it up tournament-style, with several matches of the same game happening at the same time and winners advancing to subsequent rounds until a champion is crowned. This is a particularly good option for tweens and teens and would best be held on a Saturday or a weekday on which there is no school.
- You can also consider hosting a tabletop game programming series featuring role-playing games like Magic or Dungeons and Dragons or more in-depth games like Scrabble or Monopoly. In the event of a role-playing game program/tournament, get in touch with your local comic and game stores to see if they would be interested in partnering on it and promoting it to their customers.

chapter 9

September

THE BEGINNING OF a school year can feel like New Year for families as routines and plans begin. **Healthy Eating and Meal Prep Tips** will help millennials or families save time and money as they create a meal planner. Adults in busy families may not often have a chance to explore library services for themselves, as they usually have children with them at the library. **Night Out, In** events will bring adults in for their own event while kids get to create during the same time. This combination of events may be popular enough to offer as a series, explored more in the **Power Parenting Club** in the second half of this book. **Read at the Table** offers delicious ideas to encourage all ages to read while exploring a world of flavors for new versions of book clubs. **Time Management** helps millennials especially balance work and home life as they move from school to careers and families. The September programs help all ages find more time to enjoy their lives and each other.

Healthy Eating and Meal Prep Tips

Healthy eating can seem challenging for people who are busy and on a budget, so a program that provides steps to get started is always useful.

PREP TIME	LENGTH OF PROGRAM	NUMBER OF PATRONS	SUGGESTED AGE RANGE
2–3 hours	1 hour	20–25	Millennials (great for families)

SUPPLIES/SHOPPING

- plastic food containers
- freezer bags
- scrapbook paper in various prints and colors
- clipboards (9 × 12.5" or bigger, can be found inexpensively at secondhand stores. Have enough for your projected number of patrons plus one to use as a demonstration.)
- 6 × 9" manila envelopes
- washi tape in various prints and colors
- magnet backing
- E6000 glue
- clothespins
- multicolored 3 × 5" notecards
- pens/fine-point markers
- ribbon
- scissors
- hot-glue gun/glue sticks
- rulers
- buttons, beads, scrapbooking accessories, and so on
- pencils
- individual letters used for crafting (Scrabble tiles also work well! Be sure to have plenty of M, T, W, F, and S tiles.)

ACTIVITIES

- Consider bringing in a nutritionist to speak on the topic of healthy eating well as how meal prep and planning help save time and money.

- When talking about food prep in particular, you'll want to make sure cover some specific items:

  » FDA guidelines regarding fridge and freezer storage safety
  » taking into consideration when to do food prep (what day of the week, how much time to set aside for it)

- how to seek out recipes/ingredients that work well in food prep (blogs, Pinterest, etc.)

> **PRO TIP**
>
> Pair this with the Time Management program in chapter 9 for a one-two organization punch!

Craft: Meal Calendar

1. Choose a clipboard and the desired print(s) of scrapbook paper.
2. Cover the front of the clipboard with the desired scrapbook paper, wrapping it around the edges to secure it with glue on the backside.
3. Glue one 6 × 9″ envelope to the back of the clipboard so that it can still be opened, keeping in mind to leave room for the magnetic backing.
4. Turn the clipboard over and glue magnet backing to the backside (this is only if the patron wants to be able to hang it on the refrigerator). Another option is to create a loop hook with the ribbon and fasten it to the hole in the clip of the board.
5. Once the magnets are dry (this should only take a minute or two), turn the clipboard back over and add any embellishments desired using washi tape, pieces of scrapbook paper, and so on.
6. Take seven clothespins and glue to each one letter for each day of the week (or, depending on the size, quantity, and variety of what you have, you could do the three- or four-letter abbreviation for each day).
7. Determine how you want the clips to be arranged on the board before gluing. Be sure to leave enough space between each pin to accommodate the piece of paper that each will be holding. Once you've decided, glue each pin down by one side so that the pin can still be opened.
8. While the pics dry, cut some index cards into fourths the wide way and write different meal options (each person can do this based on the things that are common in his or her household, but some standards to have on hand are "leftovers" and "dine out"). These pieces can be stored in the envelope on the back of the board.

MARKETING

- Create a display of cookbooks, especially those that deal with meal planning and eating healthy, and include information about the program. If you have already made an example craft for the meal calendar, use that in the display, and clip information about the program right on the board!

VARIATIONS

- This is a program that works well for families or adults in general, but to do this as a program for tweens and teens, consider pairing it with a back-to-school version of the Time Management program in chapter 9 and have the content be more about making healthy eating choices as opposed to meal planning.

Night Out, In

This different sort of family program lets parents attend an interesting and engaging adult program while the kids participate in an equally fun and creative one. In this iteration, parents attend a program about the library's genealogy resources while their children work on a fun craft celebrating their family.

PREP TIME	LENGTH OF PROGRAM	NUMBER OF PATRONS	SUGGESTED AGE RANGE
4–5 hours	1–1 ½ hours	10–15 (each, parents and children)	Parents and children (works well for families)

SUPPLIES/SHOPPING
- yarn in various colors
- crayons/markers/colored pencils
- hole punch
- card stock
- flower/leaf stencils
- safety scissors

ACTIVITIES

As mentioned in the description, this particular example has parents attending an informative session about the library's genealogy resources, but that is far from the only option (see variations at the end of this program).

Craft: Family Tree
(this craft is designed for children ages six to eight)

1. Using leaf and flower stencils, have the children trace and cut out a flower or leaf for each member of their families. (It's okay if they don't know or can't think of everyone! They can leave with supplies to continue the craft at home with help from their parents.)
2. Once their shapes are cut out, they can decorate each one however they choose—but be sure to include the name of the family member!
3. Once the pieces have been decorated, put a hole near the top of each.
4. Loop a length of yarn through each hole, creating a pendant that can hang from a plant or tree or as a window decoration.
5. Make sure participants leave with additional supplies if they need help from their parents completing their tree!

> **PRO TIP**
>
> Because this is essentially two programs in one, you will want to have appropriate staffing lined up. This is a great opportunity for interdepartmental collaboration between youth and adult services!

MARKETING
- Market in both the adult and youth services departments, as well as via your library's traditional means.

VARIATIONS
- *Parents and Tween or Teen Children:* Have the parents and kids work together to complete a library escape room!

Read at the Table
Delicious Book Club Variations

Book clubs can be hit or miss with libraries. Younger people may find that assigned titles for reading feels like school, and millennials may be busy with friends or prefer to discuss different titles. Very few book lovers will admit that they have enough time to read in their lives, so this activity matches fun snacks, reading suggestions, and reading time to an occasional event.

PREP TIME	LENGTH OF PROGRAM	NUMBER OF PATRONS	SUGGESTED AGE RANGE
1 ½ hours for shopping and setup	1 hour	30	Different activities are suggested per age group

SUPPLIES/SHOPPING

- plates
- cups
- plastic silverware
- snacks or treats
- napkins
- bottled water

ACTIVITIES

- *Fruit with Family*: Have a selection of cut fruit available before having youth services staff read a new picture book. Then family members have time to select books and settle to read (aloud, to each other, or by themselves) for thirty minutes.

- *Dine and Read*: Older adults may enjoy sampling international restaurants in the area. Library staff can suggest books when the registered attendees arrive whose authors match the ethnicity of the restaurant. Suggestions about books set in different regions of the United States could be offered at pubs and diners. Suggestions should include diverse US authors. The library may want to pay for appetizers or dessert for the group or the restaurant may offer to provide it if patrons are purchasing more food. Attendees are then allowed thirty to forty-five minutes of reading at the tables. This would require working with the restaurant staff or seeing if the program could use a particular section for a lunch or morning event or any night that is not as busy for the restaurant.

- *Reading and Recipes Online*: For millennials. Library social media pages could be used for an online book club where people post links to recipes on a theme, such as pies, paired with library suggestions of books with pie or cake in the title. Then participants can mention a book they are reading. This could be done at a set period each month, such as the first Tuesday.

- *Oreo Taste and Read Challenge*: For tweens or teens. During the first part of the session, teens and tweens can taste test different types of Oreos and vote on favorites before reading on their own for thirty minutes.

MARKETING

- Displays of new titles with signs featuring photos of food will help draw readers in to the event, as will frequent online posts.

VARIATIONS

- *Taste and Read*: Millennials can taste test flavored and sparkling waters or juice with fruit and cheese combos while reading for an hour. Recent titles will be available to sample and read.
- *Teen Read Week*: Have pizza brought in for an hour of silent reading. Teens and tweens can eat while reading print books or books on their phones. Bring in some recent titles for them to peruse and try.
- *Reading in the Morning*: Seniors can try different muffins, fruit, or cereals before reading for an hour. Everyone can discuss something they've recently enjoyed during the first fifteen minutes of the program before the reading time starts. New mysteries and romance or large-type titles can be available at this time before the public sees them as an incentive to attend.

> **PRO TIP**
>
> Do not be militant about silent reading time. People will still check their phones. If they are disturbing others, invite participants to spread out into different areas of the library if possible. Those who complete the reading time could be in a drawing for prizes.

Time Management

For a lot of people, time management is an evolving process, prone to adjustments and allowances for new interests, responsibilities, and commitments. Millennials in particular have been dubbed the burn-out generation (with evidence to back it up!) and are perhaps in particular need of a program that provides tips and assistance for managing the expectations put on them by themselves and others.

PREP TIME	LENGTH OF PROGRAM	NUMBER OF PATRONS	SUGGESTED AGE RANGE
2–3 hours	1 hour	20	Millennials

SUPPLIES/SHOPPING

- paper
- pens in various colors
- fine-point markers
- highlighters
- blank monthly and weekly calendar pages (this is for practice/example, so don't get too hung up on what exact month/week)
- cookie sheets from thrift stores (in good condition)—enough for your projected number of patrons plus one (for you to use as a demonstration)
- Rust-Oleum Painter's Touch spray paint in matte black (and additional colors if desired)
- two-inch-wide ribbon in various colors/patterns
- scissors
- washi tape in various prints and colors
- magnetic tape
- label maker
- rulers

ACTIVITIES

- *Bullet Journaling:* Bullet journaling is a trend heartily endorsed by devotees but can seem intimidating to some. Ask around to see if someone on staff uses this method (perhaps it's you!) and is willing to give a brief talk about it. There are also plenty of blogs/websites that break down bullet journaling and can provide a good starting place for the program.

- *Scheduling/Prioritizing Apps:* There are plenty of free apps that assist with time management/prioritizing. As with the budgeting program in chapter 4, present the options that are available. You can also ask anyone in attendance if they have tried any of them and what their experience was.

- *Incremental Time/Time Blocking:* Present the idea of breaking one's time into increments. This can be helpful when creating a daily routine as well as when balancing multiple projects. Have participants use the available supplies to practice time blocking. It might help to create a to-do list first and then use one of the blank weekly pages to fill in a plan for getting tasks accomplished.

Craft: Upcycled Cookie-Sheet Magnet-Board Calendar/Schedule for Tasks

1. Prior to the program, clean the cookie sheets as best as you can, cleaning off any caked-on materials so that the surfaces are as smooth as possible.

2. If you have the time, coating the cookie sheets with spray paint prior to the program is beneficial, as it will give them plenty of time to dry and eliminate the need for a separate open-air location in which patrons can apply the spray paint themselves during the program.

3. Using rulers and washi tape, create a seven-day grid (it doesn't have to take up the entire cookie sheet; you can leave space above and below in whatever way is aesthetically pleasing). Alternately, if a patron does not want a week-at-a-glance, they can choose to divide their board in whatever way makes sense to them. Examples: sections for work, exercise, doctor's appointments, projects, creative projects, and so on. The label maker can be used to create whatever labels the patron desires and wants applied directly to the board, or they can add an additional minor step and create them as magnets.

4. Create magnets for the board by using the label maker (or, depending on how a patron feels about their handwriting, they can use the paper and fine-point markers). Stick the label (or piece of paper) to the magnetic tape and cut to size. Encourage patrons to create whatever magnets will be most useful to them in relation to their time management: "GYM," "GROCERY SHOP," "DOCTOR," "DINNER W/ FRIENDS," and so on.

5. Cut two pieces of the desired ribbon twice the width of the cookie sheet plus a couple of extra inches and wrap each one around either end of the sheet (the sheet will hang horizontally). Secure each piece by tying a knot on the side that will face the wall/whatever it will be hung against.

6. Using the same print of ribbon or a different one depending on preference, cut a longer length that will be used as the hanger. Loop this additional piece around each ribbon end, knotting it at both. A good idea is to cut a length of ribbon that is at least two feet, tie it at one end, and then play around with how low you want the sheet to hang before knotting it at the other end.

MARKETING

- *Create a Display of Calendars/Planners:* Use old/used ones saved up from the previous year, ones that have been discarded, or very inexpensive ones bought from a thrift store. Among these items, have a book from your collection about time management, getting organized, and so on and include information about the program.

> **PRO TIP**
>
> Pair with the Healthy Eating and Meal Prep Tips program in chapter 9 for a one-two organization punch!

VARIATIONS

- *Teens:* Make the most of your iCal. The assumption here is that most teens and even tweens are using the calendars available to them on their mobile devices, which has pros and cons. The act of writing things down is good for ensuring that they are remembered, but those days are behind us, and what's most important is making sure that teens are equipped to keep track of their packed schedules by whatever means are most comfortable for them. You can do a variation on the apps portion of the main body of this program to provide them with information about additional free apps that will assist them in keeping track of various projects, assignments, and responsibilities.

chapter 10

October

FALL FUN FOR all ages can be found at the library this month. Halloween games, costumes, and even candy are not just for kids here. Help teens and tweens create and taste why, for some, Halloween is **All about the Candy.** Teens and millennials can create fantastic costumes on a dime with the educational and fun **Cosplay Event.** Costumes can work for Halloween or upcoming conventions. Help millennials and adults learn about **Haunted Happenings** in the community. And bring millennials back to **Preschool for Adults** as they craft and socialize. The library is the place for information and creativity this month!

All about the Candy

Candy is more than just a treat for Halloween. Let's get creative and do more than just eat candy (although we definitely will do that). Introduce your patrons to new varieties of candy, and turn candy into a work of art.

PREP TIME	LENGTH OF PROGRAM	NUMBER OF PATRONS	SUGGESTED AGE RANGE
2 hours	1 hour	15–20	Tweens, teens

SUPPLIES/SHOPPING

Haunted Gingerbread Houses
- Halloween music and speaker
- Pop-Tart boxes
- paper plates
- frosting (a half can per attendee—orange, purple, black, or green)
- sandwich bags
- table coverings
- plastic spoons
- plastic knives
- scissors
- candy corn
- gumdrops
- licorice
- small candies for decoration: M&Ms, gumballs, mini marshmallows, sugar ghosts or pumpkins, jelly beans, and so on
- graham crackers or gingerbread

Candy Experiments
- large bowl
- funnel
- various candy bars (snack size)
- jar of candy pieces (one of the following: M&Ms, Skittles, candy corn, Reese's Pieces, etc.)
- Coca Cola (six-pack)
- Nerds
- Pop Rocks
- balloons
- water
- choice of additional candy and soda

Candy Taste Test
- choice of international candy (available online or in international food and grocery stores)
- paper plates
- paper
- pencil
- water
- whiteboard and markers (if available)

Candy Art
- cardstock paper (large)
- cardboard
- tacky glue or hot-glue gun and glue
- candy assortment:
  » Starburst
  » Skittles
  » pull-and-peel licorice
  » M&Ms
  » jelly beans
  » gumballs
  » Nerds
  » Smarties
  » Runts

Candy Sushi
- paper plates
- plastic knives
- chopsticks
- Rice Krispie treats
- Swedish Fish
- Fruit by the Foot
- gummy worms
- jelly beans
- mini M&Ms

PRO TIP

Check with patrons to make sure no one has any food allergies before serving or handling any food.

ACTIVITIES AND CRAFTS

- Decorate a gingerbread house—in October—with a haunted Halloween theme. Put out the call to staff and collect empty Pop Tart boxes to use as houses. Buy frosting and candy decorating supplies. You can also use white or vanilla frosting and dye the frosting with food dye ahead of the program. Scoop frosting into plastic bags for teens to decorate with ease (this will also help limit their frosting consumption). Place table coverings on all tables and candy on a center table for teens to come up to and get specific candy for their haunted gingerbread house. Each attendee gets one Pop Tart box to decorate. If desired, hold a contest for the scariest, most detailed, or best decorated. Add these to a Halloween display (preferably in a closed display case, in case people decide to take a bite). Play Halloween music in the background as they decorate.

- Conduct various experiments with candy for a delicious and scientific treat.

    » Sink or float? Which candy bar sinks or floats in a bowl of water? Why?
    » How many pieces of candy are in a large jar? How can we count the pieces accurately?
    » What happens when we add Nerds or Pop Rocks to a bottle of Coke (single serving) and cover the top with a balloon? Source: www.stevespangler science.com/lab/experiments/poprocks.
    » Encourage patrons to change the variables to see if they get a different reaction. Would they get the same results with a different flavor of soda, temperature of the liquid, or candy?

- Most people have heard of Tootsie Rolls or Snickers, but have you ever tried an Ion bar (from Greece) or Kalev (from Estonia)? Taste test international treats from all over the world. You may find new favorites and interesting combinations. Pass out each candy one at a time so everyone can taste test them together. Guess which country each candy comes from and what flavors are in the candy. Rank each candy by voting together with a one-to-ten scale, with ten being the most delicious candy ever experienced. Write the rankings on the whiteboard, and pass out information about each candy tasted. Another option is to blind taste test commonly eaten candy and see if people know the differences between Reese's Pieces and peanut butter M&Ms.

- Not a huge fan of raw seafood, but still want the sushi experience? Make candy sushi—no fish required! Candy sushi can be made in a variety of ways, so get creative.

    » Cut a Rice Krispie bar in half, place a Swedish Fish on the top, and roll a Fruit by the Foot around it to secure it.
    » Cut a Rice Krispie bar so it is about one inch thick. Place your Swedish Fish, gummy worm, or any small candy in the middle. Roll the Rice Krispie bar with candy in the middle and secure it by wrapping the Fruit by the Foot around it.
    » Don't forget to taste test your candy sushi with chopsticks!

• Design beautiful works of art out of candy. Can you recreate Starry Night out of licorice? How about a self-portrait out of Starbursts? Allow students to get creative and recreate paintings or make something entirely new from candy. Buy candy in bulk, and use cardstock with a cardboard backing to keep the paper steady. Attendees should choose their image and candy (or multiple candies) and arrange their masterpiece before gluing.

TRIVIA AND OTHER FREE GAMES

• Incorporate candy trivia into your program. List candy types and guess the order in which they were invented. What does the M in M&Ms stand for? Compete to list all the candy names in ten minutes or less. Match the candy to the country it was invented in. Of course, play Candyland—regular or life-sized!

MARKETING

• Place a large covered candy jar (same as used in Candy Experiments) on the public service desk. Ask people to guess the amount, and the winner will receive the candy jar. Decorate the jar with promotional information about your program. This could also be a great social media promotion. Post a picture of the jar and ask people to guess the amount of candy in the jar. Include information about All about the Candy with your post.

VARIATIONS

• *Older Adults:* Learn about the fascinating origins of candy and how recipes have changed or stayed the same over the years. Incorporate a local history of candy if possible or candy shops. Taste test or provide a sampler of treats that were discussed.
• *Families:* Celebrate candy for all ages with Bingo and Candyland. Play candy-themed Bingo by replacing the word BINGO with CANDY. Use symbols or logos of popular candy in the columns, and use candy pieces for tokens. Play the board game Candyland—regular or life-sized! See the Fun Fair in chapter 6 for details on how to create a life-sized Candyland.

Cosplay Event/ Costume Design

Cosplay is often thought of in conjunction with fandom events, but a stand-alone cosplay program in October will appeal to comic convention attendees as well those planning their Halloween costumes.

PREP TIME	LENGTH OF PROGRAM	NUMBER OF PATRONS	SUGGESTED AGE RANGE
2–3 hours	1–1 ½ hours	20–25	Teens and millennials

SUPPLIES/SHOPPING

- scissors
- ribbons (various patterns/colors)
- fabric (5 × 5″ squares, various patterns/colors)
- white paper/cardstock
- colored pencils and markers
- old magazines, especially fashion
- duct tape (various patterns/colors)

ACTIVITIES AND CRAFTS

- If possible, invite local cosplayers (maybe you have some on staff) to present their tips and tricks for making durable costumes. Cosplayers are experts at using items found around the house to embellish their costumes and give them a unique and especially creative flair. Also consider reaching out to local fashion design programs (if there are any near you) to see if interested students would be willing to share. An additional option is reaching out to local theater troupes (community theater or school drama programs) to see if there is any interest in participating. Theater costume departments are also aces at improvising costumes!

- *Resources:* There is a wealth of information available online about using items around the house in costuming. Do some research and gather some examples that you can present to the group.

- *Brainstorm:* Put up pictures of popular cosplay subjects (various superheroes, characters from TV/movies) and ask for ideas of how attendees would put together a costume for each one using articles of clothing/accessories as well as items around the house (if applicable).

- *Crowdsource Ideas:* Ask if anyone present has a costume idea in mind. Have the group throw out ideas for how to construct that costume.

- Attendees can experiment with patterns and color combinations using the fabric and ribbons provided. Provide sheets of paper with human forms on them that patrons can sketch costume ideas on using the supplies provided.

- *Create Costume Vision Boards:* Using the supplies provided, attendees can create vision boards of costume ideas.

- *Duct-Tape Dresses:* Provide a variety of duct tape and invite attendees to practice making "fabric" out of duct tape. Visit www.duckbrand.com/craft-decor for ideas and tips on how to make dress items out of duct tape.

MARKETING

- Create a display of books about fashion and cosplay, as well as some graphic novels and fashion magazines, and include on it information about the program.

VARIATIONS

- *Tweens:* Provide items easily found around the house (empty cereal boxes, egg cartons, toilet paper/paper towel tubes, Kleenex boxes, and cardboard boxes) along with duct tape for participants to create their unique costumes! You can also put out additional items such as pipe cleaners, yarn, and puff paint.

Haunted Halloween Happenings

Halloween is more than just costumes and trick-or-treating for children; it is also an opportunity to learn about the mysterious local history in your community. Explore a cemetery and learn interesting and terrifying stories about your town. Don't have a local cemetery nearby? Not a problem. Hold an in-house program about creepy history in your state. Discover the origins of Halloween, learn your fate with a tarot or psychic reading, and of course, eat Halloween candy.

PREP TIME	LENGTH OF PROGRAM	NUMBER OF PATRONS	SUGGESTED AGE RANGE
3–4 hours	1–1 ½ hours	20–30	Millennials or older adults

SUPPLIES/SHOPPING

- blank paper
- pencils or crayons
- picnic blankets
- Halloween candy
- paper plates
- napkins

ACTIVITIES AND CRAFTS

- Speak with your local history librarian and ask them to help you present a program about interesting or creepy facts about your town. Alternate options include reaching out to your town's historical society or museum and partnering with them for this event. If possible, plan your program to take place at a local cemetery to enhance the Halloween atmosphere. Research unsolved deaths, the history of the oldest gravestone, weird occurrences that have happened in a graveyard, and so on. Share this information during a cemetery walk. Ask patrons to bring foldable chairs or provide picnic blankets to sit on, and encourage patrons to tell scary stories they have heard or creepy urban folklore. Prepare a few stories to tell yourself or read aloud from *Scary Stories to Tell in the Dark* by Alvin Schwartz.

- Teach patrons how to do a gravestone rubbing. Place a piece of paper against the front of a gravestone, and then use crayons or pencils to rub against the paper. Check with your county and state laws to ensure gravestone rubbing is not illegal in your state. Incorporate this into the scavenger hunt or as part of the cemetery walk.

- Discover if your library is haunted. Hire paranormal detectives or researchers to investigate the library and search for paranormal activity.

- Learn about the origins of Halloween and its evolution to a holiday revolving around candy and costumes. If there is a local historian, ask them to present about the history of Halloween. Alternately, one can present about the history of candy and any local connections, if applicable.

TRIVIA AND OTHER FREE GAMES

- Use horror movie trivia as a passive program or theme for a trivia night for patrons. This can include everything from the first horror movie in the genre, actor's names, or horror movies based on books or urban legends.
- Create a map (or find an existing one online) with local haunts or creepy houses in the area. Encourage patrons to take pictures in front of the homes or establishments and submit them with a time stamp to win a drawing. Make sure you have the permission of any owners to include their information and location.
- Set up a scavenger hunt in a graveyard with clues to collect. Have patrons race around the graveyard to get all the pictures they need to win the scavenger hunt. Amp this game up by asking for video answers.

MARKETING

- Include traditional images of Halloween (gravestones, candy, terrifying creatures, etc.) in flyers. Place these in your horror movie and book section at the library. Distribute them at local Halloween stores, candy shops, or the local historical society or museum.

VARIATIONS

- *Tweens:* Have a Halloween party for tweens and give them an opportunity to wear their costumes more than once. Include fun games such as guess the candy (blindfold participants and have them touch and smell individual candies to identify them), candy science (perform experiments with different candy), or Ghosts in the Graveyard, or have a costume contest.
- *Teens:* Invite a psychic to the library to tell fortunes to teens. Alternately, they can read tarot cards and teach students how to read tarot. If a psychic or fortune-teller is not available, ask an aspiring actress to "read" fortunes. Stick with positive fortunes or tarot card readings.

Preschool for Adults

Let's go back to the days when we didn't have to worry about the stresses of work and family and focus on fun! Preschool for Adults is a time to enjoy the wonders of being a kid, when life was a little easier. This is a great program to focus on creating, socializing, and meeting new people as you finger-paint.

PREP TIME	LENGTH OF PROGRAM	NUMBER OF PATRONS	SUGGESTED AGE RANGE
1–2 hours	1 ½ hours	30	Millennials

SUPPLIES/SHOPPING

- Play-Doh
- Legos
- coloring books
- crayons
- colored pencils
- washable finger paints
- cups of water for finger paints
- large finger-paint paper
- butcher paper or table coverings
- Spirographs
- selection of preschool-appropriate board games
- Shrinky Dink paper
- oven (or Shrinky Dink toaster oven)
- permanent markers
- baking sheet
- scissors
- storybooks

> **PRO TIP**
>
> Many of these supplies are found in your youth department, so ask them to borrow supplies that can be reused. If possible, use a program room that has a sink so patrons can wash their hands after finger painting and an oven to use for Shrinky Dinks.

ACTIVITIES, CRAFTS, TRIVIA, AND OTHER FREE GAMES

- Set up stations around a program room with different options for patrons to play. These stations can include finger painting, coloring, Play-Doh, Legos, and a reading corner. Include a variety of coloring-book options: coloring sheets, freehand coloring, and adult coloring books. At the finger-painting station, lay out butcher paper or protective sheets to keep the table clean. Relive the '80s and '90s nostalgia and create Shrinky Dinks or Spirographs. Make sure you have access to a sink or have hand-sanitizer wipes nearby for an easy cleanup.

- Creating a game station can also be done with games borrowed from the youth department, such as Candyland, Trouble, Connect Four, or checkers. Playground games can be done without any supplies needed and spur of the moment, such as Simon Says or Musical Chairs. Gauge your patrons' interests to see if they would be interested in having an organized game for all.

- Use your librarian skills and perform story time. Read a perennial favorite that millennials will remember, such as *If You Give a Mouse a Cookie, Brown Bear*, or *The Very Hungry Caterpillar.*

MARKETING

- Create flyers to advertise Preschool for Adults and place them in the craft and stress management section of adult nonfiction. Make them stand out by using a font that has childlike handwriting, and show a sample of different activities that will be included that invoke a nostalgia feeling for millennials.
- Consider running a concurrent program for children so stressed-out parents can attend and not worry about their child. Talk with colleagues in the youth department to see if they can run a craft or storytime that would appeal to children in all age groups.

VARIATIONS

- *Teens:* All of these activities can be used for teens, but it is a great option to offer this program during finals time or offer it as a passive program to help teens destress while they are studying. If you choose to have storytime for teens, choose a book that is more recent that they will have fond memories of, such as *Don't Let the Pigeon Drive the Bus!*

chapter 11

November

THE HOLIDAYS CAN be very stressful, and the library steps into the breach again with programs that offer fun, information, and time-saving tips. A **Coffee Shop Hop** partners the library with community eateries for a series that will warm up patrons while offering socializing and networking. Some sessions will even demonstrate fancy coffee techniques for home enjoyment or entertaining. A **Toastmasters/TED Talk/Public Speaking** class will help adults efficiently polish needed skills in today's video- and presentation-heavy environment. **Twenty Fast Appetizers and Desserts** will deliver on that title with recipes to throw together quickly for social events of the season. An **Upcycled Friendsgiving** helps millennials and older adults bring their found families together for new traditions. There is a lot to learn and enjoy at the library, as always!

Coffee Shop Hop

Patrons can get to know each other and their community through this traveling series of programs. Scale this for different ages or tie it into branch libraries with bigger systems. There are plenty of variations to enjoy.

PREP TIME	LENGTH OF PROGRAM	NUMBER OF PATRONS	SUGGESTED AGE RANGE
2 hours spent contacting area businesses and setting up	1 hour per session	Unlimited	Millennials or older adults

SUPPLIES/SHOPPING

Foam Latte Art
- milk foamers
- cups for hot drinks
- coffees

Taste Testing
- variety of flavored creamers
- variety of instant coffee packets
- hot water
- cups for hot drinks

Mug Decoration
- inexpensive (dollar store) tumblers for hot or cold drinks with paper sleeve to pull out and decorate
- markers

ACTIVITIES

Once a month, the Coffee Shop Hop will meet at the library and the other three to four weeks a month at an area restaurant or coffee shop. At the shops, people can visit, discuss books they are reading or movies they've watched, or play short trivia games.

Upon registering, patrons will receive a punch card with a list of participating cafés and shops with the dates and times of the sessions. They should all be at the same time, such as Sunday afternoon or Monday night.

Ask participating shops if members can have a discount on the day of the event or if there could be group rates.

Ideas for library sessions:

- *Foam Art:* Invite a barista from one of the shops to demonstrate how to do foam art, or get a milk foamer and have participants try to decorate their coffees and lattes.

- *Creamer and Instant Coffee Taste Testing:* Invite participants to try different flavors of instant coffee in combinations with creamers

- *Mug Decoration:* Great for a holiday session, participants can pull out the decorate-your-own-mug papers and color or draw (on the back) to have their own travel mugs.

TRIVIA AND OTHER FREE GAMES

- Have a social media page for the hop, where people can post their favorite treats or drinks at the various shops.

MARKETING

- All participating shops will carry flyers or signs advertising the events.

VARIATIONS

- Invite local police, government officials, school officials, or fire department personnel to come to one of the stops and meet community members. The library could treat the guests with coffee for those sessions.
- *Teen Café Hop*: Invite teens to have their own hop to socialize. The library could cover simple drinks for each teen per event if possible to encourage more to come.
- *Restaurant Hop*: Families could participate in a restaurant hop, including international food eateries in the area in reasonable price ranges. Rather than have set times, families could get cards punched for the highlighted restaurants.

— Toastmasters/TED Talks/ — Public Speaking

Whether you're the maid of honor preparing a speech for your best friend's wedding, a junior associate giving your first major presentation at work, or thinking about trying out an open mic night, public speaking skills are useful and stress relieving. Give your patrons a leg up at tackling their first—or next—public speaking engagement with a program tailored to alleviating their anxieties.

PREP TIME	LENGTH OF PROGRAM	NUMBER OF PATRONS	SUGGESTED AGE RANGE
2–3 hours	1 hour	15	Millennials

SUPPLIES/SHOPPING

- tables
- chairs
- refreshments
- microphone/podium
- note cards
- pencils

ACTIVITIES

Consider organizations in your area that may have trained professionals who can assist with facilitating this program: community colleges, universities, high schools, a local toastmasters group, young professionals groups, local storytelling leagues/acting troops, and so on. It is not absolutely necessary to hire a presenter for this program, but having someone who regularly leads workshops of this nature can be beneficial.

- *TED Talks:* TED Talks are presentations given by experts on a variety of topics ranging from science to business to creativity. Videos of these talks are available free to stream on www.ted.com and can provide a starting point for your program.

- *Activity:* Ted.com has a list of the twenty-five most popular talks. Choose one to show as an example—there are plenty that are less than ten minutes long, so they won't eat up too much of your program time. Have your participants critique the talk, going over what they liked and didn't like about the presenter's body language, voice modulation, pacing, and so on. Be conscious of the topic of the talk you choose to show, as you don't want your attendees to get distracted by something that may make them uncomfortable, and you don't want the discussion to veer off course by focusing on the content and not the delivery.

- *Activity:* Divide the group into smaller three- to four-person groups and ask each person to give an on-the-fly TED Talk on a topic about which they're knowledgeable. The other group members can provide feedback on how they did. After that, ask for volunteers to give their talk to the larger group, who can then also provide feedback.

- *Toasts:* An activity focusing on giving toasts is a great way to practice connecting with an audience and conveying emotion in a truthful but not exhaustive way. Some attendees may have already given toasts and will perhaps be willing to share their experiences.
- *Activity:* Follow the same procedure as TED Talks, but this time, give each person a scenario and ask them to make a toast. Example scenario: Your Aunt Carol's fiftieth birthday party. Carol is an accountant and mother of three. You spent a lot of time at her house in the summers growing up, playing with your cousins. Carol is a dog lover.

TRIVIA AND OTHER FREE GAMES

- A way to loosen up and get comfortable with the group is by playing a game of charades. Rather than pit two teams against one another, begin by asking for volunteers to come up one at a time and try to get the whole group to guess based on a clue drawn from a hat. The clues themselves are up to you, but try to stick with things that are relatively easy—the point isn't competition; it is to loosen everyone up and get them comfortable and willing to learn and try new things.

MARKETING

- Create a display of books on public speaking and include on the display information about the program. Depending on what props you have at your library, include on the display items relevant to the various venues/situations in which people give public addresses that will catch people's attention: a microphone/ mic stand, champagne flutes (empty, plastic), and so on.

VARIATIONS

- *Tweens/Teens:* TED Talks—follow the same procedure for the TED Talks previously. Ted.com also has videos of TED Talks given by and for younger people.
- *Improv Workshop:* For something that leans toward the fun and informal, consider inviting a local improv group to the library to put on a workshop for your tweens and teens. A program such as this is not only fun, but it provides an opportunity for attendees to find their voices and gain self-confidence.
- *Millennials/Older Adults:* Plan a daylong TED Talk festival in which you screen some of the most popular talks. Be conscious of what talks you choose to show. This can be a cross-promotional program for the program earlier or, depending on what talks you show, your other educational/personal improvement programs.

Twenty Fast Appetizers and Desserts

People are busy at the holidays yet often have to bring simple appetizers to parties. This program runs down easy and delicious recipes.

PREP TIME	LENGTH OF PROGRAM	NUMBER OF PATRONS	SUGGESTED AGE RANGE
2 hours to shop and prepare	1 ½ hours	30	Millennials and older adults

SUPPLIES/SHOPPING

- plates
- napkins
- bottled water
- materials to make a few of the recipes, where possible

ACTIVITIES

Plan on either showing slides with photos of these or providing samples of a few for people to see and taste.

APPETIZERS

General

- Wrap dates in slices of bacon, held with a toothpick.
- Pour pepper jelly over a block or ball of cream cheese. Serve with crackers.
- Spread cream cheese on the base of a serving plate. Add cocktail sauce, shredded mozzarella, olives, green peppers, and baby shrimp, and serve with Ritz crackers.
- Mix one cup grape jelly and one cup chili sauce in a crockpot with frozen or fresh meatballs.
- Use longer party toothpicks to hold a strip of prosciutto around a piece of cantaloupe.
- Cut pastrami or ham in thin strips and spread cream cheese lightly on one side. Roll it up with a piece of cheddar or pickle in the center with a toothpick.
- Take two slices of tomato and a thick slice of mozzarella and place on a toothpick. Make double stacks with longer toothpicks.

Mini Pizzas

- Cook canned biscuits.
- Spread with pizza sauce and shredded mozzarella, with a pinch of oregano on top, and place back in oven (still set to temperature needed for biscuits) for one minute or until cheese is melted.

Meatball Sliders

- Set meatballs on slider buns (or dinner rolls).
- Add a piece of cheddar and a sliced pickle. Hold together with a party toothpick.

Sweet Potato Rounds

- Cut ¼–⅜"-thick slices of sweet potatoes and place them on parchment paper on an oven tray.
- Brush with olive oil and bake ten minutes on each side in a 450°F oven.
- Add shredded cheddar and Monterey Jack and bake one minute more until melted. Optional: Add a small dollop of sour cream to each.

DESSERTS

Refrigerator Cake

- Layer Jell-O pudding and vanilla wafers, graham crackers, or Oreos in a bread-sized pan overnight for easy cake.

Chocolate-Dipped Strawberries

- Melt chocolate chips in the microwave and dip large strawberries.
- Add seasonal sprinkles for festive flair.

Fruit Pizza

- Spread purchased sugar-cookie dough in a pizza pan or on a cookie tray.
- Bake. When cooled, spread cream cheese over the dough and add small fruits such as strawberries and blueberries in an attractive pattern.

Festive Popcorn

- Pop popcorn and spread on a cookie sheet over parchment paper.
- Drizzle melted chocolate chips, pretzel bits, and sprinkles.
- Popcorn should be in clumps to arrange on a plate or bowl.

Peppermint Bark

- Melt chocolate and white chocolate bark separately.
- Pour chocolate on parchment paper over a cookie sheet.
- Add white chocolate, using a fork to marble the two chocolates.
- Sprinkle crushed candy canes over the top.

Easy Trifle

- Buy pound cake and cut it into one-inch squares.
- Layer them in an attractive glass bowl with strawberries and whipped cream.

Ice Cream Pie

- Purchase a cookie piecrust and add holiday-flavored ice cream, smoothing the top.
- Add crushed candy canes and Oreos to the top.

Fruit Tarts

- Purchase a piecrust and cut it into small squares.
- Place some canned pie filling (any flavor) in the center and fold corners to the center before baking kolacky-style cookies.

Oreo Truffles

- Mix two cups Oreo cookie crumbs with an 8 oz. block of cream cheese.
- Form balls to put on parchment paper on cookie tray.
- Chill. Dip balls in melted chocolate and sprinkle candy cane bits or sprinkles on top.

Mini Cheesecakes

- Make cheesecake mix.
- Add vanilla wafers to the bottom of a cupcake paper.
- Pour cheesecake mix over cookie and bake. Add fresh strawberries or candied cherries to the top.

MARKETING

- Make a handout on programs that make the holidays easier: gift craft sessions or time-saving events. Stress-relieving programs would also help.
- Invite patrons to send in their best fast appetizer or dessert recipes online for a grocery store gift certificate drawing.

VARIATIONS

- *Teens and Tweens:* Many of these recipes are easy enough to make with teens in a program, such as the festive popcorn or dipped strawberries.

Upcycled Friendsgiving

Provide fun and practical tips for your patrons to make their found-family Thanksgiving budget-friendly and stress free!

PREP TIME	LENGTH OF PROGRAM	NUMBER OF PATRONS	SUGGESTED AGE RANGE
3–4 hours	1 ½ hours	20	Millennials and older adults

SUPPLIES/SHOPPING

- empty wine bottles (enough for your projected number of attendees, plus one to use as a demo)
- discarded library books (ideally hardcover)
- paper sacks
- scissors
- X-Acto knives
- glue guns
- glue sticks
- paper
- pencils
- twine
- Sharpies
- rulers
- popcorn
- jelly beans
- pretzel sticks
- butter crackers

ACTIVITIES

Put out a display of snacks a la *A Charlie Brown Thanksgiving* to welcome patrons to the program.

- *Easy Prep Solutions and Substitutions:* Chances are your library has plenty of cookbooks based on easy food prep and low-cost, high-quality meals. Consider highlighting some books in your collection that can be particularly useful for those planning a Friendsgiving on a budget.

Craft: Recycled Book Pumpkins

This craft uses weeded-out books from your collection that are on their way to the recycling bin. Source: https://mountainmodernlife.com/diy-paper-book-pumpkins/.

1. Remove the front and back cover of the book.
2. Take a blank piece of paper and fold it in half. Draw half of a pumpkin shape, starting from the edge of the creased line. Keep in mind the size of the book you will be using so that you don't make the pumpkin too big.
3. Cut out the pumpkin.
4. Open the book about halfway and lay it as flat as possible before placing the paper template on top of the open pages with the center of the pumpkin matching up to the center binding of the book.
5. Trace the pumpkin template with a pencil.
6. Using the X-Acto knife, start carving the pumpkin out on one half of the book (on the side of the binding). Once one side is done, move to the other side. It is unlikely that you'll be able to slice through each side in one shot, but rather you'll need to cut through a few pages at a time before the side is entirely

finished. And be sure to leave an inch or two of binding coming from the top of the pumpkin for the stem!

7. Once the pumpkin is all cut out, add glue down the center of the book binding using the glue gun. Then close the two halves together to make the pumpkin shape.

8. Fluff the pages so that they form a robust pumpkin.

9. Optional: Cut out business card–sized rectangles from a paper bag to use as place cards. Use a hole punch to make a hole in one end of the card, and use twine to tie it to the stem of the pumpkin.

Craft: Wine-Bottle Table Decorations

1. Cut a piece of paper bag to wrap around the center of a wine bottle, leaving some of the glass exposed (roughly an inch or so up from the bottom of the bottle and two inches from the bottom of the neck).

2. Wrap the paper around the bottle, securing it with a little bit of glue.

3. Optional: Wrap twine around the paper for additional embellishment.

> **PRO TIP**
>
> Remove all the labels and clean the outsides (and insides, of course) of the wine bottles and jars so that they're ready to go at program time.

TRIVIA AND OTHER FREE GAMES

- *Pictophone:* Play it at the program as an example of an easy game to play at any gathering. All it requires are some small sheets of paper (cut an 8.5 × 11″ piece in quarters to cut down on the amount of paper used) and pencils/pens. To begin, everyone has a stack of sheets of paper equaling the number of people playing (eight people playing = each person has eight sheets of paper). First, each person writes down a phrase. Once everyone is done, they pass their stacks to the left. Once a person has been passed a stack of sheets, her or she looks at the phrase, moves that sheet to the bottom of the stack, and attempts to draw what is being described in the phrase. Once everyone is done drawing, the stack is passed to the left again, where the next person looks at the picture, moves the sheet to bottom, and writes what the drawing is. This alternation of drawing/writing and passing continues until each person has his or her original stack back.

MARKETING

- Put together a display of all your library's DVD collections of the TV show *Friends* as well as any movies that have to do with Thanksgiving (*A Charlie Brown Thanksgiving*). Include on the display information about the program.

VARIATIONS

- *Teens:* Have the November meeting of your teen advisory board be a Friendsgiving! Teens can make any of the crafts listed earlier to take to their own family Thanksgiving. Be sure to include popcorn, jelly beans, pretzel sticks, and crackers as well as a game of pictophone!

- *Families:* The previous crafts can work as a Thanksgiving-prep program as well. Families can practice doing one or all the crafts and take home with them the instructions so that they can create festive budget-friendly decorations for their own celebrations at home.

chapter 12

December

FESTIVE, FUN, AND relaxing are all words to describe this month's events for the library. Offer groups of different ages a chance to **Be Dazzling** as they adorn tote bags and other crafts for themselves or for gifts. Millennials can also stop in for a chance to **Destress** in between the many commitments this month may bring. **DIY Dinner Parties on a Dime** takes the fear out of hosting for millennials or older adults with interactive but inexpensive dining experiences. And **Saturday Morning Cartoons** offers millennials and older adults—or families—nostalgia and relaxation in a program that is also easy for busy staff! The library will close out another year of interactive, creative fun and helpful tips in popular events.

Be Dazzling
Artistic Adornment for Amateurs

Add bling to fun accessories at this no-sew program.

PREP TIME	LENGTH OF PROGRAM	NUMBER OF PATRONS	SUGGESTED AGE RANGE
1 hour for shopping	45 minutes	20	Tweens, teens, millennials, or older adults

SUPPLIES/SHOPPING

- fabric glue in bottle
- scissors
- Hotfix rhinestone setter set with rhinestones (you may want to purchase a couple)
- fabric markers or Sharpies
- strands of sequins (available at craft stores, can be purchased by the yard or on spools)
- craft pearls (not superlarge so they would be too heavy to glue on T-shirts or bags)
- iron-on gems
- iron, ironing surface, and board
- wax paper to put between layers of projects while painting or gluing
- coin purses (purchase from Amazon or another vendor a set of small circular canvas coin purses)
- canvas tote bags (purchase from Amazon or another vendor a set of medium-sized canvas tote bags)
- white T-shirts in a variety of sizes

ACTIVITIES

- *Coin Purses:* For teens or tweens. Use the Hotfix applicator or fabric glue to attach gems and pearls to coin purses. Or show participants how to make designs with sequins by the yard to apply with fabric glue.

- *Tote Bag Bling:* For teens or older adults. Tote bags can be decorated all over with iron-on gems, sequins by the strand, markers, and Hotfix rhinestones.

- *Neckline Bling:* For millennials. Participants can either bring T-shirts or use library-provided white shirts.

Tips on using the Hotfix applicator to decorate T-shirts can be found here: www.youtube.com/watch?v=Z3-lyMh4hug.

For this program, stones and pearls can be applied around the neckline and edges of sleeves.

> **PRO TIP**
>
> Use the equipment for several programs to get the most use out of it. Patrons could bring in their own shoes, bags, or even jeans to decorate at bling-maker events for teens and tweens.

MARKETING

- Invite creative patrons to send blinged projects including shoes, bags, jeans, and more to library social media sites. Or link to YouTube tutorials on the Hotfix applicator to encourage interest in the programs.

VARIATIONS

- *Library Technology:* Older adults may enjoy cutting lightweight fabric with the Cameo Silhouette, if the library owns it. Fabri-Tac can be applied to edges of cut fabric to seal before gluing the shapes on the tote bags and adding bling.
- *Blinged Bookmarks:* For all ages. Demonstrate how to add a few gems with fabric glue to the tops of grosgrain ribbon bookmarks at a table in the lobby. Use 1½″ grosgrain ribbon. Cut 8″ lengths at an angle on both ends or with pinking shears to avoid fraying.

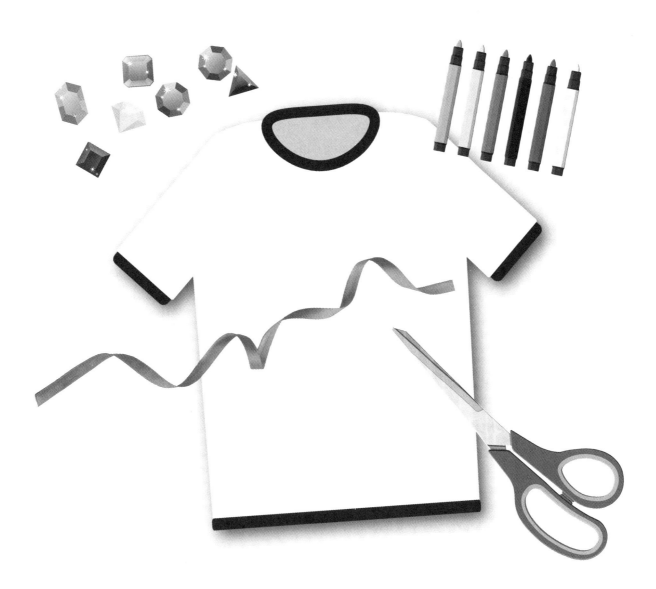

Destress and Treat Yo' Self!

In the immortal words of Donna and Tom in *Parks and Recreation*, "Treat yo' self!" Take time for yourself in this busy holiday season and enjoy a few hours of self-care. Help your patrons destress with calming, comforting activities. While everyone has different ways to destress, these ideas will be appealing to many.

PREP TIME	LENGTH OF PROGRAM	NUMBER OF PATRONS	SUGGESTED AGE RANGE
3 hours	2 hours	20	Millennials

SUPPLIES/SHOPPING

- variety of tea
- hot-chocolate packets
- paper cups
- hot-water carafe
- music player or speakers
- calm, soothing music
- cozy pillows or bean-bag chairs
- variety of classic books
- coloring books
- coloring pencils

Bath Bomb Supplies (Yields Twelve Bath Bombs)
- large bowl
- small bowl
- paper bowls (one/person)
- whisk
- measuring cups
- measuring spoons
- bath bomb plastic containers (cheap alternative: plastic Easter eggs)
- essential oils
- baking soda: 8 oz.
- Epsom salt: 4 oz.
- corn starch: 4 oz.
- citric acid: 4 oz.
- coconut or vegetable oil: 2.5 tbsp.
- food coloring
- plastic wrap

Galaxy Jars Supplies
- mason jars
- cotton balls
- acrylic paint
- plastic cups
- wooden skewer
- water
- glitter (optional)
- metallic stars (optional)

Vision Board
- poster board (one/attendee)
- magazines (to be cut up)
- fabric
- embellishments
- scissors
- glue

ACTIVITIES AND CRAFTS

- Seek out a yoga studio in your community and ask them to teach a short class on yoga basics and meditation with a focus on stress relief and breathing techniques. Alternatively, if there is a qualified yoga-trained staff member, reach out to him or her and see if he or she would like to teach the class (with management permission). Make sure you have enough space to transform a traditional programming room into an open area for yoga and meditation. Play calm or soothing music through a speaker for background noise.

- Set up a reading nook with comfortable pillows or beanbags. Provide a selection of classic children's books that patrons will remember fondly reading. Selection options can include *Charlotte's Web,* the Harry Potter series, *Pride and Prejudice, Anne of Green Gables, Where the Wild Things Are*, and *The Giving Tree.* Heat up hot water and provide a variety of teas and hot-chocolate mixes.

- Create your own spa with DIY bath bombs. Provide print instructions for patrons so you do not have to all be on the same steps. Source: www.popsci.com/how-to-make-your-own-bath-bombs.

  » Mix the dry ingredients together in a large bowl (baking soda, Epsom salt, corn starch, and citric acid). Use the whisk to remove all the clumps.
  » Mix the oil and water ingredients together extremely slowly. Divide the mixture into paper bowls among individuals. Allow participants to add their own essential oil(s) and food coloring to their bath bomb mixture (two to five drops) to personalize.
  » Stuff the mixture into silicone molds or plastic Easter eggs (a more budget-friendly alternative; participants can take them home to keep the bath bombs more intact). Press the mixture down firmly into your silicone molds of choice.
  » Let the bath bombs dry and then pop them out. Wrap them in plastic wrap to make them secure.

- Color until your heart's content and you've forgotten all about your worries. Provide coloring books (adults and children's) and coloring pencils. This can be a calm, meditative activity for people to focus on.

- Create a vision or dream board to help focus your mind on your inspirations, aspirations, and dreams. Set up a variety of magazines for patrons to cut out pictures and text to affix to their vision board. This tool helps you invest the time and energy to visualize your future and consistently reminds you of your life goals or dreams. A vision board is a very personal item, and no two will look the same.

- Create galaxy jars to create a calming nebula using everyday craft supplies. Fill plastic cups with water, and add four to five drops of paint to each cup. Lightly separate cotton balls, and fill the mason jar one-quarter of the way full. Pour the cup with the lightest color of paint into the mason jar until it soaks the cotton balls, and add glitter or stars if desired. Repeat these steps until you reach the top layer, adding colors from lightest to darkest. Use the wooden skewer to push some of the darkest paint into lighter paint and move the glitter or stars around. Water bottles can also be substituted for mason jars. Source: https://bitzngiggles .com/diy-galaxy-jar.

MARKETING

- Place flyers or handouts in test prep materials, holiday books, and yoga or mindfulness books or DVDs. Create a display of stress-relief, mindfulness, or yoga books and DVDs. If you are partnering with a yoga studio, ask them to promote the program at their studio.

VARIATIONS

- *Tweens:* Design your own fidget spinners as a way to destress and focus. Cut a template out of cardboard, place coins at the corners, use a toothpick to help it spin, cover, and decorate. Source: www.instructables.com/id/How-to-Make-a-Fidget-Spinner-Toy-Out-of-Cardboard-/.
- Create slime to keep hands busy and work out any stress. In a bowl, mix ½ c. water and ½ c. glue. Add food coloring and glitter. Pour ¼ c. liquid starch into the bowl. Stir for one to two minutes, and then knead the mixture until all liquid is gone. Make sure you check for borax allergies with parents before the program. There are also nonborax slime recipes available online.
- *Teens:* It would be beneficial to have many of these activities set up as drop-in programs during high school finals week. Partner with therapy dogs in your area (often used in Read to a Dog programs) to bring in dogs to pet as stress relief while studying. Make stress balls using rice and balloons. Each patron receives two balloons. Blow up the first one and deflate it. Use a funnel to pour rice into the balloon (approx. ¼ c.); tie off the balloon with as little air as possible. Cut off the neck of the second balloon and stretch it over the balloon with rice, tied end first so it completely covers the knot.
- *Family:* Store all negative thoughts or worries in a worry jar. Decorate a mason jar or container with fabric, stickers, or colorful paper and Mod Podge. Designate this a worry jar so children (or any family member) can write down their worries on small slips of paper and put them into the jar and come back to look at the worries after several days or weeks. Odds are that several of the worries will have passed and are no longer worries. Rip these up and throw them away.
  » Alternately, create a kindness or happiness jar for your family (or individual jars for each person) to draw from when they're feeling stressed or down. Write down positive thoughts, memories, words of wisdom, or things that make you happy.

DIY Dinner Parties on a Dime

Dinner parties don't have to be daunting. Forget timed courses and instead offer food experiences that are easier on you—and your budget. Show audience members fun options for dinner parties while they enjoy mini sandwiches.

PREP TIME	LENGTH OF PROGRAM	NUMBER OF PATRONS	SUGGESTED AGE RANGE
1 hour	1 hour	30	Millennials or older adults

SUPPLIES/SHOPPING

- plates
- napkins
- mini sandwiches (deli platter or a cut-up long sub)

PRO TIP

A representative from a grocery store may be willing to do the presentation on different options for easy dinner parties.

ACTIVITIES

- Show a presentation with ideas for different dinner party scenarios, and provide links and recipes.

- *Grill at Table:* Have an indoor luau or BBQ with a small group with these tabletop grills (available at Target or other vendors). Grilling at the table may be best on the countertop away from the eating area and near a fan, but the experience will still be fun. These recipes provide ingredients and directions for a variety of meats at a make-your-own-shish-kabob event: www.foodnetwork.com/recipes/build-your-own-shish-kabobs-recipe-1951931.

- *Pizzas:* Party attendees can choose from a variety of toppings and make individual pizzas on purchased crusts or add to sections of a large dough crust before baking.

- *Salad Bar:* Party guests can create a salad from several fresh ingredients before enjoying deli soup and purchased specialty breads.

- *Antipasto Tray:* Guests can create their own sandwiches with a buffet of toppings and fruit salad. Or hosts can make mini sandwiches with slider buns or croissants and a variety of deli meats.

- *Fondue:* Two fondue pots could be set up for guests to cook meat in hot oil in one pot while dipping bread in cheese fondue in a separate pot. Chocolate fondue for dessert is another option.

- *Taco Toppings:* Hosts can prepare a couple types of meats and provide hard and soft taco options in a buffet with toppings.

MARKETING

- Ask what the favorite go-to food for dinner parties is on a write-on or Post-it board. This could also be done on social media sites.

VARIATIONS

- *Millennials:* Go over several popular board games that dinner party hosts could offer after the meal.

Saturday Morning (at Night) Cartoons

Whether it was classic Hanna-Barbera, Disney's One Saturday Morning, Fox Kids, or any of the other varieties of animation, many of us have fond memories of plopping ourselves down in front of the TV with a bowl of our favorite cereal and turning on Saturday morning cartoons. This program is a great opportunity for patrons young and old to relive (or perhaps experience for the first time) the joys of this pastime.

PREP TIME	LENGTH OF PROGRAM	NUMBER OF PATRONS	SUGGESTED AGE RANGE
2–3 hours	2–3 hours	25	Millennials and older adults—also a great opportunity for families

SUPPLIES/SHOPPING

- cereal
- bowls
- spoons
- milk
- fun snacks
- fruit
- popcorn
- DVD player
- projector/screen

ACTIVITIES

- This program can, essentially, function as a mini festival with cartoons from different periods in time featured. Set up your spread of snacks, and hit play!

TRIVIA AND OTHER FREE GAMES

- A program that is grounded in pop culture is a great opportunity for trivia from the beginning of animation on television to today. Depending on which age level your program is aimed at, you can ask questions about the cartoons that are relevant to them. And for tweens and teens in particular, you can blow their minds with trivia about the earliest days of cartoons! Rather than have a full-blown multiround game of trivia, you can ask a few questions between episodes and keep score cumulatively or simply give out small prizes for correct answers on an individual basis.

MARKETING

- Create a display in your AV collection with DVD collections you may have as well as any related books in your collection to advertise the program.

part II

Enjoyable Clubs That Inspire and Educate

SUCCESS! YOU'VE RUN A POPULAR PROGRAM—SO POPULAR, IN FACT, THAT YOUR audience wants more of the same. Celebrate the interests and passions of the community with monthly or regularly occurring events on popular themes. Clubs offer staff a chance to run a series of programs in a similar style with some new activities for each session. This can be easier than it may sound, as sessions will likely have a set meeting time and place, and supplies may be carried over from one meeting to the next.

In this section, 25 possible clubs are featured with five activities per club, providing you with a total of 125 ideas. We expand on the clubs discussed in our previous book *A Year of Programs for Millennials and More*—adding 15 new clubs to the list and refreshing others by sharing new activities and additional variations. Clubs are arranged by themes. Tips on how to run meetings for each club are included. The ideas listed in these themed clubs should not last more than forty-five minutes to an hour. At times, outside speakers are suggested.

Each club will have the following headings:

SUGGESTED AGE RANGE
Ages that may best enjoy the events are listed here.

CLUB CONNECTIONS
In this section, tips are provided on how to run each meeting. For example, members of the 5K Club can discuss any races they recently attended or registered for during the opening minutes of their club.

IDEAS FOR SESSIONS
In this area, activities for five sessions are described.

CROSSOVER PROGRAMS
There may be other programs in this book that could have activities that would interest this club. For example, DIY Dinner Parties on a Dime may interest the Foodies Club.

VARIATIONS
Where possible, ideas for hosting club activities online or for different ages are described here.

MARKETING
Ideas for targeted promotion can be found in this section.

chapter 13

Books and Media Fun

MOVE BEYOND TRADITIONAL book discussions with new formats and ideas for different ages. The **Adult Graphic Novel Club** lets passionate readers enjoy a favorite format together. **Book to Screen** lets fans discuss big and minute changes when popular titles find their way to screens big and small. The **Bucket List Book Club** lets readers tackle titles they've always wanted to read and participate in other fun challenges. **Retro Movie Night** transports readers and movie buffs to decades past. **TV Tripping** lets audience members binge watch together while enjoying related activities. The **Young Adult Books for Next Gens Club** lets adults get together to share their passion for young adult literature. There is something for every age and type of reader or viewer here.

— Adult Graphic Novel Club —

While many adults read graphic novels without giving a second thought, plenty are still discovering that what they had previously thought was a medium "for kids" has plenty of content that is applicable to their reading interests. Encourage your patrons to give graphic novels a try with a club that encourages engagement and discussion in a "there's no such thing as a stupid question" welcoming environment.

CLUB CONNECTIONS

Of course, this club is not solely for patrons who have little experience with graphic novels but for all interested parties. Having a group that comprises different comfort and knowledge levels with graphic novels will only strengthen your discussion; in addition to hearing different viewpoints, patrons will also learn from each other.

> **SUGGESTED AGE RANGE**
>
> Millennials and older adults

IDEAS FOR SESSIONS

- *Adaptations of prose fiction: Fahrenheit 451, Kindred, The Handmaid's Tale*
- *Memoirs: Fun Home, Persepolis, Can't We Talk about Something More Pleasant?*
- *Classics of the medium: Watchmen, Maus, Blankets*
- *Award-winners: Batman: The Killing Joke, March, Ghost World*
- *Superheroes*: Try any current run of superhero graphic novels; you never know what could pique someone's interest! For a contextual tie-in, select a superhero that patrons are currently seeing on the big and small screen.

CROSSOVER PROGRAMS

- Attendees of your Young Adult Books for Next Gens Club (see chapter 13) may very well be interested in participating in graphic novel book discussions too. Be sure to spread the word at your other pop culture programs such as the TV Tripping and Retro Movie Night programs in chapter 13.

VARIATIONS

- Your local comic shop might already have a regular or periodic discussion for adults who read comics, graphic novels, and manga, so reach out to them and see if they would be interested in pairing with you for a program at the library.
- Test the waters to gauge adult patrons' interest in a graphic novel club, but include graphic novels in your already-established book discussions as well.
- Your library may very well already have a graphic novel/manga discussion for tweens and teens!

MARKETING

- Market at your other library book discussions as well via your library's traditional means. Additionally, reach out to your local comic shops and bookstores to see if you can advertise there as well.

Book to Screen

Book and movie (or television) adaptation discussion groups are a great way to reach your community and engage with a variety of people from different backgrounds. This is a simple and easy way to create a book club and can prompt lively discussions as the club reads a book, watches the movie/TV show, and holds a discussion.

CLUB CONNECTIONS

- Choose a different book and adaptation to discuss each month or semimonthly. Before scheduling any screening, make sure your library has the licensing agreement for the movie to be shown. If you're limited on time or screening space, encourage patrons to read and watch the adaptation before the program and hold a discussion at the library or off-site. If possible, create some flexibility to add a last-minute choice for a trending movie on a streaming service or a surprise box-office hit.

- Ask patrons to sign in when they enter the room. Begin the program by asking attendees what they thought of the book and movie, which version they liked better, and why. Allow patrons to discuss the merits or cons of the book and movie, and let the discussion flow. Be prepared to moderate discussions and follow up with open-ended questions to encourage people to voice their opinions.

DISCUSSION STARTERS

- What changes did they make that you liked/hated?
- Did any characters or scenes change the way you felt about the book in the movie version? Or did it resonate with you more in the book after watching the movie?
- If there is a sequel or series, will you continue on with the book or movie format?
- Would you recommend the book or movie to other people? Why?
- At the end of the program, ask for recommendations about other book-to-screen adaptations they would like to discuss.

IDEAS FOR SESSIONS

- Read a graphic novel turned movie. This is a great way to reach reluctant and younger readers. Time your discussion to correlate with the movie or DVD release to capitalize on the increased presence in the media. There are dozens of graphic novels to choose from, including works from the DC and Marvel universes, *Hellboy, Atomic Blonde, Scott Pilgrim*, and nonfiction graphic novels such as *Persepolis*.

- Focus on true crime for your book-to-screen adaptations. Read a nonfiction book and watch the adaptation as a group, if possible. The possibilities for this event are growing by the year as true crime has moved into the spotlight with adaptations or newsworthy events that reach a wide audience, such as *American Crime Story* and the discovery of the Golden Gate Killer. This is a great opportunity to include your genealogy librarian to discuss the changes and ramifications of DNA testing.

- Read and watch book-to-movie adaptations that are Oscar nominees or winners. This can be done over the course of several months as a recurring theme, choosing one adaptation for each decade or the most current year of Oscars.

- Binge watch and set up a day to feature movies or shows back-to-back. Set up popcorn and bring in comfortable chairs. Check episode run-time lengths and make sure there is enough time to screen all episodes with breaks in between. Alternately, this can be done by showing one or two episodes over a consecutive set of days, with a book-to-movie discussion on the final day.

- Read classic books and watch their modern adaptations, if you can choose which version. This can range from Shakespeare to Dickens to *To Kill a Mockingbird* and more.

CROSSOVER PROGRAMS

- Jane Austen's books would easily make a wonderful series or session for a Book to Screen Club. Her books have been adapted for the screen over the decades. Options include straightforward adaptations of her works such as *Jane Eyre* or *Sense and Sensibility* to updated versions such as *Bride and Prejudice* or *Clueless*. See Austenland in chapter 3 for additional ideas.

VARIATIONS

- This can also be modified for a teen audience: pair classic books with their YA adaptations, such as reading Shakespeare's *Romeo and Juliet* (paired with Baz Luhrmanns's *Romeo and Juliet*) or *The Taming of the Shrew* (paired with *10 Things I Hate about You*). Alternately, this club can choose classic young adult novels, such as *The Perks of Being a Wallflower*, *The Giver*, *The Outsiders*, and so many more.
- Make the film segment of the club into a podcast instead of a visual screening. Listen to true crime podcasts and pair them with a book or even newspaper articles.

MARKETING

- Place the movie posters or main characters from the chosen film into a book cover. This will capture people's attentions as they may recognize movie covers or actors and be drawn into reading the flyer.
- Add handouts to the chosen books or movies to be discussed in the club's sessions.

Bucket List Book Club

Many people have lists of books they'd like to read someday, when they have more time. The Bucket List Book Club is about making that time not just for classics but for different themed books for a fun time that will help people get to their book bucket lists.

CLUB CONNECTIONS

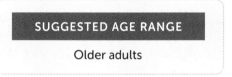

SUGGESTED AGE RANGE

Older adults

- Meetings could be held more than once during the week to appeal to different groups of adults. For example, a daytime group may appeal to retired adults, while an evening session may invite younger adults. Each meeting could start with everyone talking about something fun they've recently read and enjoyed. Coffee, tea, and some cookies and fruit may also be served—or themed treats to go with selections.
- Invite members to come with a couple questions or topics on scraps of paper. Put them in a container and draw questions. If everyone is reading different books on a theme, draw names for people to give a few remarks about their book.
- Consider limiting the group to eighteen to twenty or splitting the group into smaller groups for discussion time.

IDEAS FOR SESSIONS

- *Classics by Decade:* Each session for a few months at least could feature selections from a specific decade. Not everyone would have to read the same book. Library staff could provide a list of fiction and nonfiction titles that epitomize that era, such as *Gone with the Wind, Catch-22, Valley of the Dolls*, or *The Invisible Man.*

- *Classics by Genre:* Invite members to read classic titles from particular genres, such as an Agatha Christie or Sir Arthur Conan Doyle title for mystery or Octavia Butler or Isaac Asimov for science fiction.

- *Young Adult and Children's Classics:* Members could choose titles from a diverse list of teen's or children's award winners from the past ten years or further back.

- *Pop Culture Classics:* Many people want to read best sellers like *The Da Vinci Code* or even *Fifty Shades of Grey* but did not have the time when the book was popular. Choose a list of titles that inspired movies or television shows, and have the group vote on a few favorites for a list. This would make small group discussions fun as people converse with those who read the same title.

- *Authors:* Members could read two or more books from a list of established classic authors such as Mark Twain, Zora Neale Hurston, Maya Angelou, or Jane

Austen to discuss. This could be broken into monthlong sessions devoted to US authors, Middle Eastern authors, European authors, and more.

CROSSOVER PROGRAMS

- Read at the Table
- Austenland

VARIATIONS

- *Classics plus Movie Club:* This may appeal to millennials especially. Offer a recent remake of a classic title, such as a Jane Austen book or a Sherlock Holmes show or movie. Patrons could watch the show or movie and then briefly discuss the book.
- *Best Seller Club:* While it may be hard to keep enough copies for club members, host sessions on recent best sellers. The group could vote on upcoming titles and post the choices on social media channels rather than have them in the brochure, to be more timely and flexible.
- *Virtual Book Club:* Offer a #BucketListBookClub chat at a designated time on Twitter to discuss titles on a theme that people have read.

MARKETING

- *Books You Hated Being Forced to Read:* Make a write-on board near a display of classic titles and invite people to write titles they didn't like in school.
- *Classics You've Never Read:* Invite people to write on Twitter about classics they've never read or always wanted to read.
- Offer polls on upcoming themes or books on social media channels.

Retro Movie Night

As with trivia, there's a plethora of options for putting on a retro movie night. And as with anything dubbed "retro," there is plenty of room for debate about what fits that category. In the spirit of celebrating cultural touchstones for our patrons, we've provided some additional categories to consider when planning a retro movie night and thinking about tie-in programming.

CLUB CONNECTIONS

For a real film-lovers-club feel, provide supplemental information about each movie being shown—you can even include some trivia!

> **SUGGESTED AGE RANGE**
>
> Millennials and older adults
> (great for families)

IDEAS FOR SESSIONS

- *Oscar winners: Rocky, My Fair Lady, Chariots of Fire*
- *Sports films: Field of Dreams, Hoosiers, Rudy*
- *Musicals: Grease, Little Shop of Horrors*
- *Girl power: 9 to 5, A League of Their Own*
- *Kid power: Honey, I Shrunk the Kids; The Sandlot; Adventures in Babysitting*

VARIATIONS

- Having a movie night featuring one title is the most feasible in terms of how much time we can expect our patrons to dedicate to spending at a library program, but consider occasionally holding a mini movie fest on a Saturday, incorporating several movies under one theme.

CROSSOVER PROGRAMS

- Trivia Night—the two are practically made for each other!

MARKETING

- Be sure to market in your AV department, of course, but also talk it up at Trivia Night and any other pop culture–related programs!

TV Tripping

In today's world of streaming services and on-demand television, it might seem a lofty goal to entice patrons to come to the library to watch TV. Similar to Retro Movie Night in chapter 13, however, this program allows participants to indulge their nostalgia with an additional step of a discussion centered on the content at hand.

CLUB CONNECTIONS

- This club brings together individuals and allows them to share in their love of certain cultural touchstones. Similar to a book discussion, patrons can engage in both the entertainment itself as well as lively debate and discussion over the show featured. Particularly worthy of consideration are series that have been on for a long time and have inspired legions of fans and fandoms.

IDEAS FOR SESSIONS

- *Doctor Who:* All about everyone's favorite doctor! But wait, which doctor is your favorite doctor?

- *The Simpsons:* You could have an entire session discussing just the characters of this show, and plenty of people would probably want to!

- *Gone but Not Forgotten:* Discuss series past that have left a cultural footprint. Choose one series to focus on and the pilot episode or most memorable/standout episode from the series prior to discussion (e.g., *Friends, Firefly, Buffy the Vampire Slayer*).

- *Cartoons of Our Childhood and Today:* Similar but not quite the same as the Saturday Morning (at Night) Cartoons program in chapter 12, this session can focus on the cartoons we watched as children and compare them with their current revamps (e.g., *My Little Pony, She-Ra, Powerpuff Girls*).

- *Anime for Adults:* There are a number of series to choose from, but a place to start is with a classic series (e.g., *Dragon Ball Z, Cowboy Bebop, Ghost in the Shell*).

CROSSOVER PROGRAMS

- This topic is a natural fit for trivia, so pair it with Trivia Night in chapter 17 and theme it similarly to drum up interest in each one!
- Cross-promote with the Saturday Morning Cartoons program (see chapter 12). And theme your programs similarly if they are occurring close to each other on the calendar.

VARIATIONS

- This club will potentially draw interest from families; consider marketing certain nights particularly to families at your library.
- Tweens and teens may have a passing interest in some of the topics that come up during the run of this club, but consider having a session just for teens—perhaps to watch an episode of the original *Sabrina the Teenage Witch.*

MARKETING

- Market in your AV section.

Young Adult Books for Next Gens Club

Teen and YA novels continue to be popular among adults too. In addition to exploring the themes and genres within YA provided in *A Year of Programs for Millennials and More,* we have provided additional themes and facilitation ideas that will stretch your club members and continue to keep them engaged.

CLUB CONNECTIONS

- If you are looking to take your dedicated group of readers to the next level, the following ideas for sessions will strengthen the core of your group by featuring topics that (in some cases) carry over from one meeting to the next.

> **SUGGESTED AGE RANGE**
>
> Millennials and older adults

IDEAS FOR SESSIONS

- *Pairing with an Adult Title:* Consider pairing a YA title with a similarly themed adult novel to compare/contrast (e.g., *Outlander* and *Into the Dim*).

- *Social Issues:* By addressing social issues in a straightforward, accessible way, teen and YA novels remind us of the changing landscape of what it means to be a teenager in today's world. Go beyond "kids these days" and challenge your participants to think about how different it is for teens growing up today (e.g., *The Hate U Give*).

- *New Adult:* This was mentioned as a variation in A Year of Programs for Millennials and More, but since then, the new adult genre has gained even more traction and has proven to be a hit with patrons looking for YA-like stories with more adult content. Many authors write both YA and new adult books (Colleen Hoover, Abbi Glines, and Jennifer Armentrout), so consider even reading one of each from the same author and comparing/contrasting the two.

- *Series:* Depending on how often your group meets, think about doing a series or trilogy. You don't want the club to feel like it's dragging, so choose something that moves. In the case of the series having been adapted for film/TV, consider bringing those elements in as well.

- *Missed Classics:* Many of us are used to responding, "Oh yeah, I read that in high school," when certain titles are mentioned, but just as many will respond, "Ah, we didn't read that one at my school!" Take a survey of your regular attendees to see if there are any commonalities in titles that they didn't read in school and never got around to going back to (e.g., *The Grapes of Wrath, The Great Gatsby, Their Eyes Were Watching God*).

CROSSOVER PROGRAMS

- Consider a week or two of "back to basics" programming that includes Preschool for Adults and Camp Nostalgia and occurs around the time of a meeting of this club!

MARKETING

- In addition to promoting this club at your other library book discussions, be sure to talk it up at any like-minded nostalgia-based or millennial-targeted programming (see those mentioned earlier).

chapter 14

Parenting

YOUNG FAMILIES NEED libraries and attend programs often, but those parenting teens or intergenerational families could use assistance also. A club for **New Parents** introduces the library and services to young families or to teen parents. **Parenting Teens** offers help to those navigating career and college prep as well as teen social and emotional issues. The **Power Parenting Program** series offers ideas for a club for parents and grandparents that meets at the same time as programs for youth.

Welcome to the Library
A Guide for New Parents

This series of programs could be reoffered periodically for new parents or parents new to the library. Community organizations could have special, condensed versions of sessions for new teen parents, new adoptive parents, ESL parents new to the area, and more variations. If enough came to the programs and wanted to continue, it could form into a New Parent Club with monthly sessions on library services.

CLUB CONNECTIONS

- Meant as a weekly series of three sessions initially, this group could begin with tours of different parts of the library. Parents would be allowed to bring children or babies with them to this event, so sessions should be no more than thirty to forty-five minutes. Coloring sheets and colored pencils could be offered to children older than babies.
- Give each family a book log to record reading minutes from everyone. People who have read an hour together by the last session can get another book as a prize.

IDEAS FOR SESSIONS

- *Welcome Packet*: Plastic book bags with a picture book and library card applications plus a family reading log can be given to each family. If a family has multiple children, provide multiple books. At this first session, tour the youth department and read a book aloud to children with a fingerplay or song. Give tips on reading aloud to children.

- *Library Cards*: Help families get library cards for children or themselves and tour the computer services, international materials area, and media departments, as they may be popular stops for parents. Give coupons for an extra hour at a computer or a dollar off fines or another bonus.

- *Introduction to Programming*: Go over popular youth programs and upcoming family events. Give each family plain card-stock bookmarks, and help them stamp a fingerprint from everyone to decorate.

- If the group wants to continue meeting, demonstrate a library service and offer a short storytime or music at future meetings. For example, a staff member from the readers department could discuss book clubs and adult reading programs, or someone could discuss computer classes. Offer some interactive toys that can be washed in between sessions.

CROSSOVER PROGRAMS
- Power Parenting Club

MARKETING
- *Spreading the Flyers:* Information about sessions could be sent to community organizations including hospitals, religious institutions, park district buildings, the YMCA, and more.
- *New Baby Bags:* Packets of basic library information in book bags could be stocked at area hospitals with a board book, library card applications for family members, and basic information on services for families.

Parenting Teens

Some may feel this group should be called Surviving Teens, but this could be a space for parents to learn about recent issues that could affect their family at short programs.

CLUB CONNECTIONS

- At most meetings of this club, parents could sign up for library e-mail newsletters as they come in and pick up flyers about recent adult programs. Speakers could help with topics

  for sessions, including local law enforcement, therapists, community college representatives, or even library staff. Sessions should be short, no longer than forty-five minutes. A teen craft or entertainment program could run at the same time so parents may want to stay. No one is required to register or come to each session, encouraging adults to come to what may be sensitive topics.
- Invite parents and community organizations to help provide ideas for sessions.

IDEAS FOR SESSIONS

- *Vaping, Smoking, and Town Laws:* Laws are rapidly changing to keep up with the dangers of vaping. Parents could see samples of dab pens, Juuls, and the latest paraphernalia from law enforcement and hear about what might happen if teens are caught with items on their person or if they are using them.

- *Learning Social Media:* Library staff could go over basics of Snapchat, Instagram, and other social media that the teens in the area are using.

- *Helping Your Teen through Tough Times (Such as Breakups, Suspensions, Trouble with Friends, or Trouble with Grades):* A local therapist who specializes in adolescent or family counseling can provide tips on what to watch for in terms of teen depression and anxiety with hard life events and strategies to support teens going through them.

- *Options for the Future:* When teens do not want to go away for college. Community college representatives can discuss trade or different career options for teens who do not want the four-year college experience away from home.

MARKETING

- Ask schools, religious organizations, law enforcement, and local counseling centers to help promote this club and series.

—Power Parenting Program—
Parent Nights

The Parent Nights Club offers busy parents a way to talk to each other and learn about what the library can offer them while young children are playing nearby or doing a craft at a table in the room. While it may not always go smoothly every time, what program does?

CLUB CONNECTIONS

SUGGESTED AGE RANGE

Older adults

- Sessions of this group will be casual, allowing for parents to get up and help young children with needs. Allow parents to bring healthy snacks and drinks for young children. Having a coloring table with puzzles and paper to draw and color may help entertain younger children.
- Meetings can begin with introductions of parents and children. Staff can then introduce the theme for the night with a short demonstration of a library resource, complete with handouts—for example, how to download audiobooks or take language classes online through the library website. Staff can also sign up families for summer or winter reading programs and help connect families new to the library with staff who can get their library cards made.

IDEAS FOR SESSIONS

- *Meet Local Preschools and Day Cares:* Invite staff from local preschools and day cares to introduce themselves to the families and give an overview of their facilities.

- *Parks, Zoos, and Inexpensive Family Fun:* Library staff can show photos or discuss local places families can visit for low or no cost—including an overview of upcoming family-friendly programs.

- *Food Trends:* Invite an area doctor to discuss food allergies and what to watch for in children before showing parents library cookbooks for all kinds of diets. Or invite a chef who can demonstrate making simple baby food or peanut-free snacks.

- *CPR or First Aid:* Invite someone from the fire department or a medical professional to show basic first aid and the Heimlich maneuver for helping choking children. If desired, parents could sign up for a CPR certification at a time when they can be without their children.

- *Kid-Friendly Home Tips:* Invite someone from a home repair store or someone in construction to show ways to affix bookshelves to walls, ensure screens do not pop out of windows when pressed, and other tips on making homes safe for children.

chapter 15

Passions

WHERE BETTER CAN people try or pursue passions and hobbies than in a communal group at the library? These clubs offer a place for people of all ages to pursue dreams and passions. The **5K Club** helps those who want to run races share tips and reach goals. **Crafterwork** allows social times while learning different art forms. **Foodies** celebrates flavors and culinary achievements, while **Historical Activities** educates people who want to experience the past. Those who want to pursue crafts from past decades will enjoy the **Retro Craft Club**. Budding actors will find support and lessons at the **Story and Performance Troupe**, while those who dream of publishing will work with others in the **Writer's Workshop.** Patrons will be inspired while they enjoy themselves in these clubs.

5K Club

Lots of people like to get fit or have running a race as one of their goals, but not everyone has the money or time to go to a gym. People who like to—or want to—run 5Ks come together in this club to share news on races and fitness gear and to encourage each other. This club offers tips and camaraderie on the road to fitness.

CLUB CONNECTIONS (FROM *A YEAR OF PROGRAMS FOR MILLENNIALS AND MORE*)

SUGGESTED AGE RANGE
Older adults

- Each meeting can start with members mentioning races they have completed, evaluating the course, crowd, prizes, and overall experience. Members in attendance can also discuss any upcoming events for which they are registered.
- At the first meeting patrons attend, offer water bottles and pedometers as welcome gifts and inspiration to keep going with their fitness journey.
- Members who have run or walked their first 5K can receive an inexpensive medal, and celebrating other milestones, such as completing five races or a longer race, can help motivate club members to keep returning.

IDEAS FOR SESSIONS

- *Balance and Core Strength:* Invite a local trainer from a studio or park district to show simple stretches to improve balance and core strength, including ones that can be done sitting at work or through daily activities at home.

- *Gear and Protection:* Invite a member who runs many races or someone from a sporting goods store to discuss clothing options, including higher-tech clothing for winter workouts. Discussions can include the best sun block for athletes.

- *Music and Audiobooks for Workouts:* Show members how easy it is to download music and audiobooks onto devices from the library website to enliven workouts. Discuss options for devices and headphones for working out. Another activity for this session could involve organizing a library virtual 5k fundraiser. (See variations for ideas.)

- *I Finished a 5K, What's Next?* Discuss options for longer races or triathlons, and have a local trainer discuss how workouts can be increased to change race types.

- *Local Workout Options:* Favorite walking and running paths in the area. Members can discuss workout paths in the area, showing routes on a projected map. Indoor workout spaces for walking or running should also be discussed and evaluated by members.

CROSSOVER PROGRAMS

- Healthy Fixes would appeal to members of the 5K Club who are working on overall fitness.

VARIATIONS

- *Virtual 5K Club:* Mentioned in *A Year of Programs for Millennials and More,* the Virtual 5K Club can have a dedicated Facebook page or tab on the library website. Members can send in information about 5Ks they've completed, with information about the races.
- Another option is for themed virtual 5Ks each month. When members complete walking or running the distance of a 5K, they can send in the map of their workout from an app to receive an inexpensive themed medal each month.
- *Charity 5K Club:* Organizations in the area in need of funds can be the host of a monthly virtual 5K. People who participate, send in $10–$15, and walk or run the distance over a period of weeks get an inexpensive prize and help raise funds.

MARKETING

- Feature members of the 5K Club on social media, emphasizing that all levels of fitness are welcome. Members can be pictured with medals from area races or with the club water bottle, along with information about the next meeting.
- *Stepping Off Fines:* Walk ten thousand steps in the library challenge. Patrons who keep track of their steps in the library over the period of a month can get their fines cleared. Information about this challenge can be posted with information about the 5K Club.

Crafterwork

Personalize your life and enjoy a creative outlet with crafting after work at the library, or Crafterwork. No matter the medium, crafting is a fun, low-stress hobby that allows one to be imaginative and incorporate art into their everyday lives.

COMMUNITY CONNECTIONS

- Invite club members to share their creative passions and if they have a preferred medium. Encourage them to share the last craft project they worked on and what crafts they would like to try in the future.

> **SUGGESTED AGE RANGE**
>
> Millennials

IDEAS FOR SESSIONS

- *String Art*: Create designs with push pins, canvas, and string (or embroidery floss). Patterns can be created with push pins outlined from patterns online or arranged however the crafter chooses. Outline the shape with string, wrapping it twice around the corners, and fill in the shape with string by crisscrossing and wrapping from pin to pin. String Art can also be done with a piece of wood and nails.

- *Sip and Paint*: Enjoy a glass of sparkling grape juice—or wine if your library has a liquor license for those twenty-one and over—while painting a beautiful piece of scenery or cityscape. Display the designated image on a large screen, and play music in the background. Consider painting the picture before the class so patrons have an example on hand.

- *Calligraphy*: Learn about hand lettering and different ways to incorporate calligraphy into your life. This could come in handy for card making, wedding or birthday invitations, and general handwriting improvement. Be cognizant of different forms of calligraphy, which vary by culture.

- *Customized Wooden Sign Painting*: Create a fun new piece of signage to add to a home or bedroom. Preprint letters in various typography and popular phrases for homes or seasons for patrons to trace and paint on wooden boards. Examples: "There's no place like home," "I love fall most of all," and "__'s Room." Treat or stain light or unfinished wood one week before the program.

- *Craft Supply Swap*: Designate drop-off days and times for slightly used or new craft supplies that people want to donate. Supplies can range from fabric to canvas to beads. Crafterwork Club members or volunteers can help organize the supplies by medium. Hold the swap day a few hours or days after the last drop-off session and allow all to attend.

- *Pinterest Night:* Choose one or two popular Pinterest crafts for everyone to make. This could include perennially trending crafts such as mermaid tails, Scrabble tile necklaces or coasters, candle making, or mason jar crafts.

CROSSOVER PROGRAMS

- *Upcycled Friendsgiving:* Create upcycled crafts for Friendsgiving based off of items in the Craft Supply Swap. Also, you can create a beautiful Friendsgiving sign in the wood painting session.

VARIATIONS

- Create a parent-and-child or family crafting session. Include crafts that both a parent and child will enjoy.

MARKETING

- Create a prototype of a few program sessions and design a display to advertise the program and craft books. Encourage patrons to draw or add their own flair to a display. Display examples from previous crafting programs and upcoming Crafterwork sessions.
- Include flyers advertising Crafterwork in the nonfiction crafting section.
- Poll patrons about their favorite crafting activity or medium to incorporate into future programs.

Foodies

As the name suggests, a club for Foodies at the library can be a variety of things, from educational to social. The group can visit ethnic restaurants, sample international dishes for holidays, or learn to make quick, trendy things on their own. While this club will work for a variety of ages, ones for teens or millennials in particular can be especially appealing for those groups—no pun intended.

CLUB CONNECTIONS

- A short demonstration video from a food show can be playing as members come in. This could vary each meeting according to the theme of that session.

> **SUGGESTED AGE RANGE**
>
> Teens or millennials

At each meeting, members could discuss a visit to a restaurant they enjoyed or a snack or meal they made and particularly savored. Each session should involve a vote on favorite and least favorite aspects of the activity, as well as plans for future meetings. If the programs need to be published well in advance, the group could brainstorm for the next season of programs.

IDEAS FOR SESSIONS

- *Around the World Tasting:* Depending on local offerings, the group could meet at different international restaurants in the area for a few sessions. Or samples of different foods could be purchased and brought in for the group. This may be especially fun around holidays of other cultures, including Diwali, Bastille Day, winter holidays, and more.

- *Gourmet Upgrades:* Show club members fancier ways to make favorite treats. This could include additions to mac and cheese or peanut butter and jelly, unique waffles, or ultimate grilled cheese sandwiches. Make enough so club members can sample the treats.

- *Yogurt Parfaits and Protein-Filled Snacks:* Ask athletes or local grocery store staff for tips on good protein snacks, and offer materials for club members to make yogurt parfaits. Also offer tastings of various labeled protein bars, and discuss which has the most sugar and which are truly the healthiest.

- *Vegetarian Delight:* Find vegetarian alternatives either frozen in the grocery store or prepared from local restaurants, and invite the club to sample. This may include meatballs, tofu, and other popular substitutions. Discuss how people managed with Meatless Monday recipes from World War I and II, and share some recipes.

- *Fruit and Cheese:* For millennials, it may be possible to offer very small samples of wine with different fruits and cheeses. For both teens and millennials, slice popular fruits and cheese and have members sample different combinations. Be sure to include dried fruits too.

CROSSOVER PROGRAMS

- DIY Dinner Parties on a Dime
- Healthy Fixes—Substitutions That Taste Great
- Salty and Sweet Fest
- Cooking with a Waffle Iron
- DIY Frozen Drinks and Desserts
- Twenty Fast Appetizers and Desserts

VARIATIONS

- If the group is going to meet at different restaurants, it could focus only on that and have a different name versus one that meets in the library to prepare snacks and easy recipes.
- If the library has both teen and millennial foodie groups, only one shopping trip for both would likely be needed, and the setup would be the same for both groups with some small adjustments for different tastes and interests. Two programs could be created with one theme and planning.
- Tweens may be interested in some of the topics such as gourmet fixes or yogurt parfaits for occasional foodie sessions. It is a good way to gauge interest for topics when those patrons become teens and want to join the Foodies group.
- Older adults may enjoy a History of Food Club with visits to area wineries, organic farmers markets, and more. They may also enjoy sessions featuring food invented during certain time periods or decades such as Depression-era foods, Fabulous Fifties BBQ, or Watergate-nicknamed foods from the 1970s.

MARKETING

- For teens, Foodies members can demonstrate a new snack or discuss their club at the beginning of other food-related programs to inspire more teens to attend.
- Offer recipes and links on library social media to go with the theme of that month's Foodies. Be sure to include plenty of pictures.
- Invite members of the clubs to do live or recorded short videos with themes and to discuss future themes. Videos showing members enjoying themselves at the library and in the community help advertise the event to attract more members.

Historical Activities

An hour-long monthly club meeting is hardly enough time to sample the Renaissance or to learn about the Ming dynasty, but it can give members a taste of periods in international history with samples of fashion, sports, music, art, crafts, or even food.

CLUB CONNECTIONS

- As members enter the room, they should receive a handout with clues about the activities. Each session will begin with a short introduction to

the featured time period, with either music playing or a brief presentation with visuals of some highlights. The same headings, such as fashion, sports, music, and art could be covered at each meeting so members get used to the format, with a food to be served at the end. Each session should involve three to four activities. These can be done either at rotating stations for small groups or for the entire group to work on together. At the end, invite members to check out materials featuring the time period of the next meeting.

IDEAS FOR SESSIONS

- *Madcap Mid Century*: Play rockin' music as people enter, and show a movie of dance steps for a jitterbug as people come in. Invite interested members to try it.

    » Create soda fountain drinks with small amounts of seltzer water or soda and ice cream or banana splits with yogurt and other fruit.
    » Show members how to do simple flower loom crafts, a macramé bookmark, or pom-poms.
    » Play music from Woodstock.
    » Build with building sets a la Tinkertoys/Erector sets (for families).
    » Discuss dolls and collectibles from the midcentury with adult groups.

- *Ming Dynasty*: Discuss the rapid changes in leadership and the influence of trade both in and out of China during the Ming dynasty.

    » Members can try simple wood-block painting or stamping.
    » Members can try to write their names in Chinese lettering from looking at a sample alphabet.
    » Make a simple true-or-false test with details about the Great Wall, such as how long it is, how long it took to build, or what repairs were made during the Ming dynasty.
    » Show examples of porcelain and fashions from this time. Examples of paper cutting and folding could be copied by club members on inexpensive origami paper.
    » Offer fruits and vegetables as a snack.

- *Renaissance:* Play harp or lyre music if possible while members enter and then give a brief presentation in important paintings, scientific discoveries (astronomy), music, and literature.
    - » *Weapons:* Duels became popular starting in this period. Discuss weapons used with photos and famous duels in history (Hamilton/Burr).
    - » *Chain-Mail Bookmark:* Though chain mail is usually found in weaponry or gear, it can also make attractive bookmarks or bracelets. Club members can fashion these smaller items with circle jump rings and pliers.
    - » *Flower Wreaths:* A good activity for families, wreaths can be made with silk flowers, ribbon, and flower wire or tape.
    - » *Printing Letters with Stamps or Blocks of Type:* The printing press helped move books and literature far ahead during the Renaissance. Show club members how to print letters or simple designs onto paper with ink.
    - » *Measurements and the Vitruvian Man:* With tape measures, invite groups of members to decide if Da Vinci's Vitruvian Man was accurate.

- *Egyptian Adventures*
    - » *Hieroglyphs:* Show examples of Egyptian hieroglyphs and invite small groups to draw a message in that code. Pass the messages to the next group to have them solve it. This site has great examples for the alphabet: https://discoveringegypt.com/egyptian-hieroglyphic-writing/egyptian-hieroglyphic-alphabet/.
    - » *Fashion:* Beautiful jewelry adorned men and women in ancient Egypt. While much of it was elaborate and large, have club members try to attach an Egyptian charm (search under that term in Amazon or at craft stores) to a premade chain necklace with some beads.
    - » *Pyramid or Sphinx Building:* Puzzles are available to build a Sphinx, and Lego kits for pyramids are also available for fun small-group activities.
    - » *Food:* Serve figs, dates, cheese, and bread for this meeting.

- *Native Americans*
    - » Which settled in the area of the library? Or in which regions?
    - » *Learn Some Language:* The Mohawk language is described here with some words and links to other Iroquoian languages: www.omniglot.com/writing/mohawk.htm.
    - » *Art and Crafts:* Show photos of sand painting, bead looms, or metal etching, or invite club members to make simple necklaces with silver charms, turquoise, beads, and leather cord in honor of many tribal styles.
    - » *Native American Drumming:* Get a recording of Native American drumming or watch a YouTube that explains the beats. Club members can drum with their hands on a table or their laps in a circle to try some of the rhythms.

CROSSOVER PROGRAMS

- Medieval Magic
- Austenland

VARIATIONS

- *Holidays through History*: In the weeks before international holidays—such as Diwali, Spring Festival, New Year, Boxing Day, or other events that are possibly new to patrons in the United States and Canada—offer a Holidays through History event with dance, music, simple crafts, and speakers from those countries to discuss how the events came into existence and how they are celebrated now.

MARKETING

- A display of materials in the time and culture of the next club program will help advertise the event, along with samples of the crafts.

Retro Craft Club

Help participants revisit fun past arts and crafts in this casual club. It takes planning, shopping, and possibly practicing time, but the emphasis here is on memories, not on the skill of the staff. Members may want more than one session to work on projects or to explore more projects with a particular skill.

CLUB CONNECTIONS

- Members will begin meetings by introducing themselves and discussing what they like to make.
- Staff can then show a video or demonstrate the skill for that session.
- Everyone should leave with instructions and links to tutorials, if applicable. Members may need to take home materials (like the latch hooks) to finish.

SUGGESTED AGE RANGE

Older teens, millennials, and families

IDEAS FOR SESSIONS

- *Button Bracelet*: Participants can bring in flat buttons with two or four holes, or buttons can be purchased from craft stores or thrift shops.

  » Purchase .7-mm elastic cord, scissors, and craft glue.
  » Buttons are threaded on the cord through the holes and knotted to form a bracelet. Glue reinforces the knot. Directions can be seen here: www.youtube.com/watch?v=2lIZtUpI7X4.

- *T-Shirt Bag*: Participants or the library can supply sleeveless T-shirts or regular T-shirts.

  » Purchase fabric markers and fabric scissors (sharp).
  » Easy directions can be found here: www.mommypotamus.com/no-sew -t-shirt-tote-bag-tutorial.
  » Sleeves are cut off and then a fringe is cut on the bottom of the shirt before it is knotted to seal the bottom and turn the shirt into a tote bag.

- *Leather Crafting*: Leather bookmark kits are available at many craft stores or online.

  » Purchase several decorative stamps.
  » Have a block of wood and a hammer available to facilitate the stamping process. The wood goes underneath the leather project, and the hammer lightly taps the stamped design into the bookmark.

- *Decoupage Boxes or Frames*: Purchase Mod Podge Fast Dry, decorative lightweight papers, and inexpensive wooden frames or boxes. Paintbrushes and table coverings will also be needed.

  » Everyone can tear the paper into smaller pieces or cut them before affixing them to frames or boxes with Mod Podge in layers.

• *Latch Hook*: Latch hook tools can be purchased for as little as $5 from online or craft outlets. Other supplies include latch-hook canvas, Sharpies, and paper (for underneath canvas when drawing design).

» Mini, complete latch-hook kits purchased online can be an easy project, though members will likely need to take them home to finish.

CROSSOVER PROGRAMS

• Ideas can be transferred from this group to the Crafterwork sessions.

VARIATIONS

• Any one of these activities could be a program by itself or tied in to reading program themes. Teens or tweens would enjoy making the tote bags or button bracelets especially.
• Families could work on the decoupage frames.

MARKETING

• Make samples of the crafts for photos and displays, or demonstrate one of the crafts in short videos for library social media.

Story and Performance Troupe

Shine the spotlight on acting, reader's theater, and more with a Story and Performance Troupe at the library. Encourage patrons to step out of their comfort zone and engage in storytelling, drama, improvisation, comedy, and the world of acting.

CLUB CONNECTIONS

SUGGESTED AGE RANGE

Tweens, teens

- If there is a closed-door program room available, hold meetings in this space away from an audience of family members or patrons. Clear out all tables and chairs except for one or two to take advantage of the full room, and use the occasional chair and table for props. Ask students why they joined, what they hope to accomplish in the club, and a favorite movie/play/comedian. This can help steer the direction of activities in sessions and guide which plays or books are chosen.
- Acting and being on stage takes a lot of confidence, and it's okay if not everyone is prepared to be front and center. Be encouraging and don't worry about the varying abilities of students. Have fun and help each student gain confidence in front of an audience or grow their skills backstage. Things may not go according to plan, but that's half the fun as students learn to act, public speak, and adapt quickly in new or frequently changing situations on stage.

IDEAS FOR SESSIONS

- Film book trailers for popular or upcoming books. Shoot promotional commercials to market programs. Ask schools to play them on morning announcements or in the cafeteria, include them on digital marketing in your library, or add them to your library's social media.

- Put on a short play for younger children or families in the library. This could be a weeklong or series workshop that culminates with a performance for young children and family members. Assign roles or audition students for speaking roles. Don't forget about all the behind-the-scenes work such as directing, scenery, makeup, and costumes. This is a great precursor to community or school plays and a chance for teens to find their niche in the theater world whether on stage or behind the scenes.

- Learn how to storyboard or screenwrite. How do you set the stage and tell a story from beginning to end? Print storyboard templates, and screen a movie short. Have teens storyboard what they just saw to determine the narrative arc of the story and learn how to find important details. Split the club into groups to create a story in six panels or less using blank templates. Bring everyone back together and have each group act out their story. Encourage constructive criticism and get feedback from the audience: Did each scene make sense? How could the story arc have changed? Was there enough emotion? Did all characters connect and make an impact in the story?

- Set up a storytime for club members to perform in front of an audience. Members can act out the story as you read it to an audience of young children. Ask students for storytime favorites, choose roles (or even switch them out throughout the story), and practice acting out scenes for the next storytime. See if a student would like to help read the story aloud with you. Depending on the age group of your storytime, stay in the back of the room to read while the actors perform the actions front and center. This can also be done with puppets or even flannel boards.

- Pare down an award-winning children's book to ninety seconds or less. Author James Kennedy created a filmmaking contest called the 90-Second Newbery (http://90secondnewbery.com). Alternately, choose a favorite book that many have read and will recognize. This can be a wildly creative process as you (and your club members) narrow down the best, most random, and funniest moments from a children's book into a script to film. Add a theme, combine mediums, switch out actors—the possibilities are endless!

- Play improv games that will help actors break the ice, listen to each other, create fun and engaging storylines, and form a cohesive scene. Here are a few game examples:

  » *Actor Switch Out*: Draw a situation/scenario from a hat, and get a character from the audience. Three actors start the scene and have a cohesive conversation until someone yells "Switch!" An improv member taps one of the actors on the shoulder, takes his or her place, and resumes the conversation or changes the direction of it entirely.

  » *Lines from a Hat*: Write down random, disconnected sentences on scraps of paper and place them in a hat. Have the actors in a scene draw sentences and find a way to work all the phrases into the scene.

  » *Word Ball*: All actors stand or sit in a circle and begin to throw a ball to each other. Person A starts with the ball and says a word (example: *kitten*). He or she throws the ball to the next person, and he or she says the first thing that comes to mind about Person A's word (response: *fluffy*). Person B throws it to the next person, who responds to the word *fluffy*. This is an easy way to break the ice and get students to think and react quickly.

CROSSOVER PROGRAMS

- *Austenland:* Take the magic of Jane Austen and turn it into a film in ninety seconds. Another option for adults is to have a community theater play based off of one of Austen's novels.

MARKETING

- Create flyers or posters with drama masks, a spotlight on stage, or a red curtain. Distribute the flyers at community centers or schools. Connect with the drama or music teachers at middle or high schools in your service area to see if they can recruit students or give you a few minutes to promote your program.

Writer's Workshop

This club inspires writing creativity and helps authors prepare their work for publication. By providing critiquing, camaraderie, and helpful information about the business of writing, this group will meet the needs of new and experienced authors. It should be age-specific for content reasons.

CLUB CONNECTIONS

SUGGESTED AGE RANGE

Tweens, teens, millennials, or older adults

- As people arrive, they can sign up to participate in the critique portion of the night. When the group is settled, everyone can introduce themselves and say what they are working on so everyone can see that all levels of writers are present.
- The themed activity will be next, followed by the critique section. For that part, people can read one to two pages, and everyone who wants to can make a positive constructive comment or two. It may be a good idea for staff to go over how this part of the group is handled before the first person reads.

IDEAS FOR SESSIONS

- *Writing Goals:* At any point in the year, authors can adjust their goals and look at what they've accomplished already that year. People can discuss anything that particularly helped them achieve a goal.

- *Timed Sprints:* Set a timer for fifteen minutes and invite everyone to write on paper or on laptops. At the end of the time, count the words and discuss. This is a great way to show writers how much they could get done even with thirty minutes to an hour of writing each day. Extrapolate it to how many days it would then take to complete a twenty-thousand-word novella or seventy-five-thousand-word book.

- *Queries and Synopsis:* Bring samples of queries and synopsis and invite people to work on their own for this activity. Point out strengths of samples, and highlight library resources to help with this.

- *World Building:* Have the group discuss genres, authors, and stories with excellent world building, and why it was effective. Bring samples of famous science fiction, historical, or fantasy titles, and read paragraphs from some as examples. Invite people to write details of a fictional world on paper for this activity.

- *Fan Fiction:* Have everyone choose a show, movie, or book series and plot out a new story for that world in a few paragraphs. Discuss online outlets for fan fiction.

VARIATIONS

- An online version of a writing group is possible with adults in a closed Facebook page or Yahoo group. Rules should be made clear about ages and how critiques work. Library staff can still post tips and activities on themes every week or month, and critiques can be handled.

MARKETING

- Host at least one meeting in local cafés if possible a year to help promote the group, or make information about the group widely available at cafés, bookstores, and community groups. Contact local chapters of the Mystery Writers of America, Romance Writers of America, and the Society of Children's Book Writers and Illustrators about critiques, and invite members from those groups to speak briefly at a Writer's Workshop meeting at the library about their groups.

chapter 16

Skills and Service

ONE OF THE BEST services the library offers patrons of all ages is teaching skills through materials and programs. But learning new skills can definitely be fun. Those skills can benefit others through some service-themed clubs too. In the **Community College Connection**, library staff can partner with community colleges to reach adults young and old, showing the best of what the library has to offer with interactive events. Adults can learn new crafts and make things for those in need through the **Crafting for Charity** group in the library. A **Job Skills** club can always help those going for their first job or embarking on a new career. The **Service Club** section suggests projects for patrons to do to help the community. A **STEAM Club** combines science and technology for younger patrons, while **Tech Night** helps young adults or older patrons learn about new trends.

Community College Connection

Having a continued partnership with your local community college is a great way to keep in contact with the school and patrons once they are past their teen years. Community colleges can provide great insight into higher education initiatives and upcoming events. Go beyond traditional library programming and focus on keeping connected with the student population at the local community college with innovative and targeted programming.

CLUB CONNECTIONS

Use a combined method of ten- to fifteen-minute drop-in programs and dedicated programming. This is a winning combination to reach the community college crowd. Be flexible and hold some programs off-site at the college.

IDEAS FOR SESSIONS

- *Zen Garden Workshop*: Design a desktop Zen garden to use for peaceful thoughts in moments of stress. Add playful mini figure toys such as dinosaurs, unicorns, or Lego characters to your Zen garden.

- *Have a Pi Day Celebration and Competition on March 14*: Compete with other students with two-minute basic math worksheets (addition, subtraction, multiplication, etc.).
  - » Sample different flavors of pie and tally each student's favorite on a large whiteboard in a common area.
  - » Play Pie in the Face against other students and see who gets pied first.

- *Are College Students Smarter Than Fifth Graders?* Set a math competition for the afternoon or evening and encourage fifth graders and college students to compete against each other. This is a great crossover with the STEAM club for tweens.

- *Cookie Decorations*: Decorate cookies during finals week as a stress reliever and a tasty snack. Gingerbread men are an easy decorating item, just provide frosting, decorating gels, and candy add-ons.

- *Card Making with Quilling*: Design cards for all occasions in this session. Borrow stamps from the youth department and provide stickers, markers, colored pencils, and card-stock paper to create cards for every occasion. Teach patrons how to quill (folding paper into tiny shapes and adhering them to the front of cards) to add an extra flair to your cards.

- *How to Find a Job When You're in College*: How do you search for a job when you have little professional work experience in your designated field of study? Set up a networking meeting to create a support system of other community college students looking for leads and jobs. Organize résumé assistance for patrons and job searching tools.

- *Bad Art*: Don't make it look nice! Nothing fancy or frilly—it's time to get creative and silly. The point is for the art to be so bad it's almost comical. Buy paintings at secondhand stores for attendees to add objects, paint, collage, and more. The worse it is, the better the Bad Art!

CROSSOVER PROGRAMS

- College students are busy as they balance school and work. Help them achieve some stress relief at the Destress and Treat Yo' Self program in chapter 12.

VARIATIONS

- Create student care kits. Remind them of the value of their public library and the many ways they benefit from having it in the community.
- Challenge community college students to get a library card. Set a goal for the library card drive and offer a pizza party at the college—first come, first served. If possible, run the challenge in September for National Library Card Month.

MARKETING

- Promote the club at school and the public library. Invite the Student Services Department to assist, offer advice, and promote the club. Discuss club opportunities with community college librarians as well, and ask them to place flyers or posters in the school library.

Crafting for Charity

Help people cope with challenges and struggles in life through crafting. Crafting is an expressive medium that has amazing healing powers. Attendees will learn new ways to craft and help people with their art.

COMMUNITY CONNECTIONS

Ask attendees if they have ideas for ideas for crafting and special causes that are near to them. Find ways to incorporate new mediums and charities. Reach out to local shelters and ask what items the club could provide, such as artwork to brighten hallways.

> **SUGGESTED AGE RANGE**
>
> Tweens, teens

IDEAS FOR SESSIONS

- *No-Sew Blankets*: Make blankets out of fleece for shelters or Project Linus, which donates blankets to children going through cancer or serious diseases. Fleece blankets can be any size and require no sewing. Measure out the two pieces of fleece/blanket and lay them back-to-back with the patterned side out. Trim the excess so they are even; cut three- to four-inch squares from each corner. Cut a three-inch fringe around the blanket and knot the pieces together.

- *Color a Smile*: Color pictures to send to anyone who needs a smile. This organization sends pictures to senior facilities, the military overseas, and anyone who needs a smile. Print pictures to color here: https://colorasmile.org/volunteer/coloring-pages-instruction.html.

- *Plarn*: Make a mat for the homeless from plastic grocery bags—otherwise known as plarning. This project can be done with or without crocheting. Organize the bags by color and style to create a pattern. Cut the bottom and top of each bag off, removing the handles. Accordion-fold the bag so it is about one inch long. Tie three bags together in a braid and leave a tail to tie the next braided bags to. Form a tight circle and work outward until you have the right size for your mat. Place wax paper on one side and iron to fuse the braids together. Source: www.instructables.com/id/How-to-Make-a-Rug-from-Plastic-Grocery-Bags/.

- *Scarves for Charity*: Provide scarves for the needy. Knitting scarves is a great knitting or crocheting beginner project. Once you have mastered scarves, try new patterns for hats or mittens. Items can be left at the library for anyone in need of scarves or donated to Warm Up America (http://warmupamerica.org).

- *Artwork*: Create a colorful collage, mural, or mosaic and donate it to a local charity group. This artwork could be displayed or auctioned to provide funds for the charity.

- *Pillowcases*: Create vibrant pillowcases for children going through serious illnesses. Decrease their stress while in the hospital with colorful homemade pillowcases. Ryan's Case for Smiles has specific instructions for the creation and care of the pillowcases: http://caseforsmiles.org.

CROSSOVER PROGRAMS

- Any program that has a crafting element can benefit from this club's activities. Both Crafterwork and the Retro Craft Club can implement these wonderful ideas.

VARIATIONS

- Establish an intergenerational crafting-for-charities program. Teens and tweens can partner with seniors to create crafting projects. It would be fascinating to discuss the differences in crafting today versus in decades past.
- Create a community crafting challenge in the library. Encourage everyone who enters the library to decorate a quilt square to create a quilt for a local charity. Set a challenging but attainable goal based on your service population. Pick a date for a large-scale quilting program in your library to make dozens or hundreds of quilts.

MARKETING

- Create samples of these crafts and display them at public desks. Promote your club on social media and show students in action, letters from charities donated to, and information about your next meeting. Place Crafting for Charity flyers in craft books.

Job Skills

Many teen patrons have entered or are preparing to enter the workforce, where they will learn and develop many useful and fundamental skills. This club will look at particular aspects of the workforce and provide teens with an opportunity to ask questions and receive valuable information. Consider pairing with a local organization that assists in job training and placement to facilitate this program series.

CLUB CONNECTIONS

- Teens will enjoy a judgment-free space with their peers as they get ready to enter a new phase of young adulthood.

SUGGESTED AGE RANGE

Teens

IDEAS FOR SESSIONS

- *Job Searching*: Besides "now hiring" signs in windows and word of mouth, how do you know who's hiring and for what?

- *Interviewing*: Before needing to use job skills, one must first have interview skills. Hold a session in which interview skills are the topic of conversation. You can even have the group do practice interviews.

- *Professionalism and Accountability*: No matter where one's first job is, it is never out of line to conduct oneself with respect and professionalism. Whether it is punctuality, courtesy, honesty, and respect, the earlier these skills are developed and put to use, the better.

- *Customer Service*: Nine times out of ten, a person's first job is working in some form of customer service. Librarians can attest that customer service can bring with it the occasional challenges and frustrations but that the lessons learned and experience gained in those positions are invaluable.

- *Volunteering*: While not providing a paycheck, volunteering provides useful and practical experience that will carry over in an individual's life. Spend a session discussing volunteer opportunities in your community, and if possible, invite some representatives from organizations to provide more information.

CROSSOVER PROGRAMS

- Pair with the Résumé/Cover Letter Writing program in chapter 8 for a well-rounded start on entry (or reentry) to the workforce.
- Teen Job Fair in chapter 3—hold a session of this club that will help students prepare for the Teen Job Fair.
- This program is one that is also well-suited to a program in the Adults Facing Social Challenges club in chapter 17.

- With an income comes the responsibility of making decisions with one's money. Pair a job-skills session with the program Making Budgets Less Taxing in chapter 4.

VARIATIONS

- With slight tweaking, this club is just as relevant to adults seeking to enter or reenter the working world.

MARKETING

- Be sure to cross-promote at the programs mentioned earlier as well as at local schools in addition to your library's traditional means.

Service Club

Keep up the momentum in your service club and become even more visible in the library and community. This club teaches people more about what the library does and its role and importance in the community.

COMMUNITY CONNECTIONS

- This club is a great way for patrons to see their work in action and how it can benefit their town.

IDEAS FOR SESSIONS

- *Welcome Basket*: Create welcome baskets for people who just moved to the area and got their library card. Decorate the basket and add information about the library and a treat or promotional material. Include anecdotes about the library, memories, or how much the library means to the community.

- *Read-a-Thon*: Celebrate the library and host a read-a-thon. This can be great to correspond with National Library Week, promote a referendum, or celebrate Banned Books Week.

- *Community Garden*: Plant a community garden outside of the library. Sign up for shifts to water, weed, and harvest. Donate the produce to local food banks.

- *Mural*: Create a mural for the lobby, program room, or cafeteria. This can be a collage of everything great about the library, an abstract painting, or more. Work with marketing if your club wants to create a photo collage to find the best pictures to represent the library.

- *Kindness Rocks*: Use paint pens or bright acrylic paint to write kind words of wisdom. Have the rocks line the path of the library sidewalk, or create random peaks of color in rock beds. Some suggested phrases:

    - » "You are awesome!"   » "Be brave!"
    - » "Inspire!"   » "You are beautiful!"

CROSSOVER PROGRAMS

- The Crafting for Charity Club activities will appeal to many Service Club members who want to expand their crafting skills.

MARKETING

- Promote the Service Club at board meetings and Friends of the Library meetings. Some people who attend board meetings may be looking for ways to give back to the library and are interested in attending this club. Hand out flyers to job agencies, ministries, or volunteer associations for people looking to volunteer in their community.

STEAM Club

Science, technology, engineering, art, and math—you know the acronym: STEAM. This educational initiative opens the doors to many program opportunities (and gives your club the extra buzzword). Many youth services library programs already align with one or more of these standards and can be tied into your club. Use inquiry-based learning for self-discovery and allow students to guide the activities to determine how and why things operate. STEAM gives library staff the freedom and flexibility to cover any aspect of STEAM and do it on the cheap.

CLUB CONNECTIONS

SUGGESTED AGE RANGE

Tweens

- Invite students into the program and ask them what excites them about STEAM and if they have a favorite subject based on STEAM. In the beginning of your first few meetings, give a reminder of what STEAM is and how it is present in our everyday lives. Introduce the activity or experiment you will work on in the session. Ask students to think about which subject area of STEAM it covers (usually more than one). After the initial activity, ask how the experiment or activity can be changed and what they want to learn from changing it, and go forth with the new and improved activity. After the student-modified activity, ask what they learned from it and how it can apply to their lives.

IDEAS FOR SESSIONS

- *Engineering Challenge*: Develop critical thinking and design skills with these challenges.

  » Build a tower out of paper that can support a basketball.
  » Create a platform of paper cups and cardboard to support one team member's weight, leading to a discussion of weight distribution.
  » Build a boat that can float out of paper, scissors, and tape. Use a kiddie pool or water table to test each team's boat.

- *Pendulum Painting*: Create colorful designs with a homemade pendulum out of PVC pipes, twine, and a cup. Tie three pieces of PVC pipe together, creating a teepee, and from that tie three pieces of twine that hang a few inches off the ground. Cut a small hole in a cup for paint to drip through, and attach the cup with binder clips to the twine, allowing tweens to change the height. Use the pendulum to paint designs on large pieces of construction paper, and have discussions about motion and gravity.

- *Light Painting*: Capture the contrails of light in a dark room using a camera or phone, glow sticks, and flashlights. Use a long-exposure setting on a digital camera, or download a long-exposure app. Use flashlights with a deflated balloon pulled over the headlight or glow sticks to create light trails. Tweens can create designs, words, and more. Discuss why this happens only with a long aperture, change the settings, and experiment.

• *Coding*: Learn about coding basics with whatever tools you have at your disposal: Raspberry Pi, Scratch, or robots such as Dash and Dot or Lego Mindstorms EV3. Scratch is a free download from MIT, while the others vary in price. Set challenges for each person to complete before the end of class: moving forward a certain number of paces, turning 360 degrees, changing direction when there is an object in your path, and so on.

• *YouTube Science*: Test out popular YouTube science experiments to see if they work and discuss why or why not.

  » *Egg Walking*: Is it possible to walk on top of eggs in an egg carton? Does it work without the carton, with a different type of carton, or with shoes? How is it possible if the eggs are so easily cracked? Set out tarps, buy multiple cartons of eggs, and be prepared for a mess.
  » *Elephant Toothpaste*: Which ingredients and materials created a reaction? How did the elephant toothpaste change with different materials and quantities?

CROSSOVER PROGRAMS

• *Night under the Stars*: Tweens or families can use many of the science activities in Night under the Stars: creating a sundial, using robots to help the Mars Rover, and determining constellations and stars.

VARIATIONS

• Change the club to a STEM club or focus on only one of subject areas in STEAM.
• Create a STEAM club for adults that are interested in learning more about the world they live in. Parents may also be interested in this club to help their children in these subjects.

MARKETING

• Highlight the advantages of the STEAM club at local elementary and middle schools. Promote the STEAM club at school board meetings, PTA meetings, and with teachers. Reach out to teachers to seek their advice and partnership, and see if students can get extra credit for attending.

Tech Night

Hold a program series that helps your patrons understand the technology resources at their fingertips and in the library that will help them in school projects, creative hobbies, and potential careers.

CLUB CONNECTIONS

- Choose one resource to focus on at a time and explore it in however many sessions you deem necessary/appropriate. Patrons can choose to join for one specific miniseries, or some may attend every session.

IDEAS FOR SESSIONS

- *Podcasting*: One of the most popular formats by which both professionals and amateurs are getting their content out into the world is by means of a podcast. At its essence, a podcast is an easy thing to create, but finding effective means of recording for a clean, well-produced podcast may not necessarily be at everyone's disposal.

- *3-D Printing*: Give your patrons an in-depth look at how 3-D printing works and the details necessary in creating schematics for a 3-D printing project.

- *Creating a Website*: There any number of free ways to create a website, but what goes into planning a website? What is/isn't important to include on the home page and each subsequent page? What about font/color choices?

- *Recording Music*: Similar to Podcasting, this is something done easily enough using minimal resources, but an elevated recording session requires tools that the library (when and where possible) can provide.

- *Coding Basics*: Present the basics of common coding languages (Ruby, Python) to assist patrons in their technological endeavors.

CROSSOVER PROGRAMS

- Pair with Creating Your Story in chapter 4 to delve more into the role of social media in the earlier topics, such as Podcasting and Creating a Website.
- Also consider pairing with a program on Game Design (see chapter 1) to explore options for creating video games at the library.

VARIATIONS

- The content of the sessions can/will vary slightly for a younger audience, as their needs and interests will be slightly different, but the opportunity to present library resources is the same.

MARKETING

- Market this program in both your teen and adult areas, depending on which audience a particular session is directed toward. It may be necessary in some cases to hold nearly identical sessions—one for tweens and teens and one for adults.

chapter 17

Social or Game Time

THE LIBRARY IS a great place to connect for **Adults Facing Social Challenges**, and we have ideas for those patrons to enjoy in particular. Those patrons of different ages who want to enjoy gaming of all kinds can meet for fun activities in the **Gamers Guild** or during **Trivia Nights.**

Adults Facing Social Challenges

The library as a resource for all members of our community will always be our primary charge. Adults on the autism spectrum continue to be vulnerable after they have aged out of the support systems available to them while in public school and can benefit greatly from library programs designed and facilitated with them in mind.

CLUB CONNECTIONS

- Adults Facing Social Challenges is presented in *A Year of Programs for Millennials and More* as a one-off program, but there are plenty of topics and themes for potential ancillary programs to warrant it being a regular or semiregular occurrence or even a club.

- Success of this club or series will be largely dependent on collaboration and partnerships with organizations in your community that serve/work with this demographic. Having someone who works with this demographic partner with you and be present at programs is important.
- Aim for a balance of informational sessions about skills and topics relevant to attendees and fun, recreational programs.

IDEAS FOR SESSIONS

- *Dating/Social Etiquette:* This is a topic that can be uncomfortable for anyone but is useful for everyone. Ask your community partners for recommendations of a qualified individual to lead a session that is both casual and informative and provides patrons a safe space to ask questions. It is important that this session not be perceived as condescending or patronizing.

- *Book Discussion:* Consider occasionally peppering in a book discussion. Solicit interest and suggestions of titles/genres from your patrons.

- *Adult Coloring Night:* Turn on some chill tunes and provide some snacks while your participants color and socialize.

- *Game Night:* Have one big game of charades/Pictionary or provide several games in case smaller groups of attendees want to try out different things.

- *Job Skills:* Similar to a Dating/Social Etiquette program, ask your community partners and other organizations in the community for recommendations of a qualified individual to lead a session that is both casual and informative.

CROSSOVER PROGRAMS

- Incorporate elements of the Crafting for Charity Club in chapter 16 for a meeting that combines fun, service, and learning new skills.
- Everyone loves a movie night! Don't forget to advertise the meetings of your Retro Movie Night series from chapter 13.

VARIATIONS

- This same programming series can be replicated for tween and teen patrons on the spectrum as well, and just as with adult patrons, your first step will be checking to see what other resources/organizations are available to these patrons in your community and at school to inform how you go about planning and facilitating your programs.

MARKETING

- In addition to advertising via your library's usual means, reach out to organizations in your community that serve this demographic to see if they will help get the word out. Be sure to advertise your programs for adults facing social challenges at all your adult programs, and vice versa.

Gamers Guild

Gaming has the amazing power to bring people together as they search for clues, solve riddles, and enjoy a fun dose of healthy competition. Games can be appreciated and enjoyed no matter your age, economic status, or gender. Encourage your patrons to try new games, learn together, and discover new ways to game with a club dedicated to gaming.

CLUB CONNECTIONS

- Encourage patrons to sign in when they walk in. Do a quick icebreaker question and ask patrons what their favorite game is and why they enjoy it. This is a great way to gauge patrons' gaming interests and see if they prefer competitive games, cards, role-playing, and so on. Many of these games can be used for upcoming sessions. If patrons show enthusiasm for a particularly unique game, ask the patrons to lead the future program and guide the gaming session.

- Set up gaming stations at multiple tables and give an overview of each game or the type of games. Ask patrons if they have played any of these games before, or make sure that rules are readily available. Divide up the time at each station by the number of games, but have flexibility if attendees want to continue/finish their game. Make sure to circle the room and help patrons with gaming questions or clarifications. Enjoy the time and play a game with patrons. Be prepared for gaming to go a little beyond the program time allotted to finish up games. Allow patrons to continue to play in the louder zones of the library after the program.

IDEAS FOR SESSIONS

- Play only card games for this session. Encourage patrons to share favorite card games and teach other attendees. This is a great opportunity to allow patrons to take a leadership role, share their knowledge, and learn new games. Make sure you have multiple card decks on hand and instructions for card games you may be unfamiliar with. Some ideas for card games: Crazy Eights, Rummy, War, Slap Jack, and more. Include specialty playing card decks such as Uno, Exploding Kittens, or Old Maid.

- Make it all about the dominoes! Divide into teams and see which group can create the longest or most intricate domino run in an allotted time (fifteen to twenty minutes). Create mini challenges such as including a level change from a table to the floor or including two rows of dominoes. Playing the traditional game of dominoes or one of its many iterations is also encouraged.

- Multisided dice, storytelling, and an active imagination are the only things necessary for a night of RPGs (role-playing games). Dungeons and Dragons (D&D) is one of the most well-known versions of RPGs, but there are one-time adventures that can be played in a single session. Check out https://rpggeek.com for inspiration or one of the many D&D handbooks. Be prepared to be a game master (GM) and frame the beginnings of the storyline. If there is a high interest in RPGs, consider creating a separate club or series for an extended, continued adventure that will last more than one session.

- Go beyond playing old-school board or video games from the '80s and '90s. Learn how children and adults entertained themselves with games from decades or centuries ago. This can include yo-yos, chess, backgammon, charades, Monopoly, Tiddlywinks, marbles, jacks, Bilboquette (cup and ball attached by a string), Game of Graces (stick and hoop racing), and so on.

- For millennials and older adults, consider harkening back to childhood days and enjoying a night of party games from their youth, perhaps those you would find at an elementary school party. Ideas for games include pin the tail on the donkey, hide-and-seek, Bozo buckets, hopscotch, and musical chairs.

- Does your library have virtual reality (VR) equipment? Put your VR technology to good use and theme a session around VR gaming. This is a great chance to introduce your virtual reality technology to patrons who are unfamiliar with its wide ranges and to bring in VR fans to your Gamers Guild.

CROSSOVER PROGRAMS

- *Tabletop Game Night:* Invite Gamers Guild members to help with your Tabletop Game Night—after all, they are the experts! Poll them to see what tabletop games would be best to include for different age groups and to moderate games if needed.
- *Game Design:* Creating games is a great way to celebrate gaming for a group of gamers. By giving attendees the freedom to design their own games, library staff get to learn about their interests and chosen playing styles. Gamers Guild may even have new favorite games to play after this.
- *Fun Fair:* Ask your Gamers Guild to build large-scale versions of board games for all to enjoy at the Fun Fair for families. See chapter 6 for more details.
- *Preschool for Adults:* Incorporating nostalgia-centered childhood games is a natural tie-in when planning a Preschool for Adults program. Create a new station or set aside group gaming time to play some classic childhood party games.

MARKETING

- Advertise and promote Gamers Guild at a local gaming store. If possible, see if they are available to partner or share ideas about new or popular games.
- Leave out a game such as checkers or cards at the public service desk with a flyer for Gamers Guild. If someone starts to play or shows interest, make sure to promote the Gamers Guild. If your library circulates games in house or for check out, place promotional flyers in the game.
- Tie in a gaming program with International Games Week. Encourage the club to host games they have built or created (large scale, board, or otherwise). This is a great opportunity for tweens and teens to learn about library programming, cooperation, planning, and logistics as they learn how to plan a library program for others.

Trivia Nights

This monthly social program is a frequent favorite among patrons, but it can stand to be refreshed every once and a while so that patrons don't get bored and lose their desire to keep coming back. Additionally, a particular theme might catch a novice's eye enough to inspire them to come and give it a try. Here are some additional themes to keep your trivia night fresh!

IDEAS FOR SESSIONS

- *Local Trivia:* Each town, no matter how big or small, has a history. Sometimes the smallest towns have the most history.

- *Science Fact and Fiction:* Switch up a science-themed trivia night by interspersing some questions about the equally mind-blowing genre of science fiction!

- *Sitcoms:* From *All in the Family* to *Modern Family*, there are plenty of did-you-knows about this particular subset of television history.

- *Boy Bands:* Before you dismiss this as an '80s/'90s fad-focused theme, remember that technically, the Beatles were a boy band.

- *Harry Potter:* You'll want to be careful about getting too niche in themes so as not to alienate a number of your participants, but Harry Potter has reached such near ubiquity that it's at least worth a try.

CROSSOVER PROGRAMS

- *Saturday Morning Cartoons:* As mentioned in the Saturday Morning Cartoons program in chapter 12, there is a wealth of anecdotal information regarding the history of animation that lends itself well to a trivia night. Consider giving your regular trivia night an animation theme to help in promoting your upcoming Saturday Morning Cartoons program.
- *TV Tripping:* This series can easily incorporate trivia nights on its own, but you can enhance each program by connecting it with a specially themed edition of your regular trivia night.
- *Treat Yo' Self:* The idea and reasoning behind this program (see chapter 12) comes from the sitcom Parks and Recreation, so it's a perfect tie-in with a sitcom-themed night of trivia!
- *Cosplay/Costuming:* This program in chapter 10 is included in October programming for a reason.
- *Sing-Along Movie Night:* There's more to know about these movies than the lyrics to the songs!

MARKETING

- As we've seen, Trivia Night itself can be great marketing/promotion for other programs, and vice versa, particularly when the themes/topics of each are related.

About the Authors

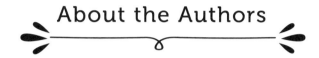

AMY J. ALESSIO is an award-winning librarian with a black belt in karate. Her latest book is the coauthored *Pop Culture–Inspired Programs for Tweens, Teens, and Adults* (American Library Association, 2018). Her fiction includes the Amazon best-selling Alana O'Neill mysteries with vintage recipes and romance novels under another pen name. She teaches graduate-level young adult literature and webinars on book trends and social media. She is a romance reviewer for *Booklist*. Learn more at www.amyalessio.com.

KATIE LAMANTIA is a collection development librarian at Baker & Taylor. She previously worked as a teen librarian at the Schaumburg Township District Library in Schaumburg, Illinois, and is a former teen advisory board member turned teen librarian. She is the coauthor of the books *Pop Culture–Inspired Programs for Tweens, Teens, and Adults* (ALA Editions, 2018), *50+ Fandom Programs: Planning Festivals and Events for Tweens, Teens, and Adults* (ALA Editions, 2017), and *A Year of Programs for Millennials and More* (ALA Editions, 2015). She has a personal and professional appreciation and interest in pop culture and has presented at multiple state and national library conferences about libraries, teens, and programming for patrons in their twenties and thirties. In her spare time, she enjoys traveling, reading, writing, and extreme adventure activities.

EMILY VINCI is the fiction manager at the Schaumburg Township District Library in Schaumburg, Illinois. Her professional interests are promoting the acquisition and appreciation of comics and graphic novels in libraries as well as working to make sure that patrons see themselves and their experiences reflected in library collections. She presents frequently about pop culture and niche library programming and coauthored the books *A Year of Programs for Millennials and More* (ALA Editions, 2015), *50+ Fandom Programs* (ALA Editions, 2017), and *Pop Culture–Inspired Programs for Tweens, Teens, and Adults* (ALA Editions, 2018). A lifelong lover of the pop culture of the '70s, '80s, and '90s and an avid collector, she currently has more than two hundred copies of the Jurassic Park films on VHS and is always looking for more.

Index